THE ARIZONA

BUCKET LIST
EXPLORER

Your Essential Travel Guide to Uncovering Epic
Landscapes and Unforgettable Experiences

ALDEN GARCIA

MAPS & IMAGES AT YOUR FINGERTIPS!

Download your bonus at the end of the book

Table of contents

Your Ultimate Guide to the Grand Canyon State

Every kind of traveler, from families looking for excitement to couples seeking romance to solo adventurers wanting solitude, will find what they're looking for in this comprehensive guide to Arizona.

With information about lodgings and unique encounters in this extraordinary nation, this book is more than just a collection of facts; it is a treasure trove.

This guide gives you the opportunity to experience Arizona's breathtaking scenery, lively culture, and rich history through seven comprehensive itineraries that may be adjusted to fit any budget. Making sure everyone has an enjoyable journey, each route is designed to be easy to follow and full of interesting things to see and do.

One special thing about this guide is the digital version that comes with it as a bonus. I am more dedicated to protecting the environment with this edition. Only the digital version, featuring all of the breathtaking photos, is accessible in order to minimize paper use and contribute to the preservation of as many trees as possible. Not only does this help the environment, but it also gives you access to high-quality color photos and downloadable PDF maps that you can keep on your favorite device.

Get ready for an unforgettable, eco-conscious journey through Arizona like no other, guided by an expert who will make every stop along the road an unforgettable experience. This book has everything you need for a once-in-a-lifetime vacation, whether it's with the family, a significant other, or just yourself.

How to Use This Book

For anyone seeking to discover Arizona in special and significant ways, this book serves as an all-inclusive guide. This book is structured to be easy to follow and packed with information that will be useful at every stage of your trip.

Structure and Content

The guide is divided into chapters corresponding to different geographic areas of Arizona and includes detailed itineraries that cover both major attractions and hidden gems. Each itinerary is described day by day, providing a detailed schedule that includes:

- *Accommodations: options for each stop, suitable for all budgets, complete with prices and contact information.*
- *Dining: suggestions for breakfast, lunch, and dinner that reflect the local cuisine, with options for all tastes and budgets.*
- *Activities: daily experiences that will enrich your stay, from culture to nature, detailed with prices and duration.*

Each itinerary is designed to be flexible; you can follow it day by day or use it as inspiration to create your personalized route. The variety and completeness of the details will ensure you have all the necessary information at your fingertips, for a stress-free and discovery-filled journey.

QR Code for Digital Edition, Maps and Images

At the end of the book you will find a QR code that allows you to download the digital edition of the guide. This version includes not only all the text of the paperback but also enhances the experience with downloadable maps and color photos of the locations described. Using the digital edition is the perfect way to have quick and easy access to maps while traveling and to enjoy beautiful images that will make you fall even more in love with Arizona.

Chapter 1: Exploring Arizona's Natural Wonders and national parks

1.1: The Grand Canyon: A Journey Through Time And Nature

The Grandeur Of The Grand Canyon

Envision yourself at the brink of the Earth, as a tale unfolds that has been simmering for billions of years. The Grand Canyon is one of the most breathtaking natural sights in the world, thanks to its enormous size and breathtaking variety of rock formations and colors. Not only is it a canyon, but nature has been painting this massive canvas here from the beginning of time. Sunset, when the sky lights up in shades of orange and pink, or daybreak, when the light overflows over the brink, either way, you're reminded of the earth's immense power and beauty at this location.

Geological Marvel

Explore the Grand Canyon's strata, where each layer reveals a story from Earth's history. Canyon walls display a geological mosaic formed over millions of years, with black, dense Vishnu Schist and durable, cliff-forming Kaibab Limestone among the many stones. The layers that make up the canyon are geologists' paradise because they include more than just rocks; they document Earth's natural history

Ecological Diversity

The Grand Canyon provides a safe haven for a dizzying array of flora and fauna, all of which have evolved to thrive in the extreme conditions found within the canyon. Elk and mule deer find sanctuary in the verdant ponderosa pine forests that line the canyon's edge, while tenacious cactus and heat-loving reptiles populate the desert scrub at the canyon's foot. Once on the verge of extinction, the majestic California condor now gracefully flies over this natural bastion.

Recreational Adventures

The Grand Canyon is a veritable adventure playground for anybody who can't resist the outdoors. Get your heart racing by rafting the turbulent Colorado River, descending the famous Bright Angel Trail, or any combination of these exciting activities. With every twist and turn of the river and route comes breathtaking panoramas and the exhilaration of discovery.

Cultural Significance

Tribes like the Navajo and the Havasupai hold this magnificent terrain in the highest regard because of its deep connection to Native American culture and history. A trip to the canyon is an opportunity to feel at one with the natural world and the many civilizations that have called this area home for generations.

Conservation Efforts

Maintaining the Grand Canyon for the benefit of future generations exemplifies our persistent resolve to do just that. As we take in the canyon's breathtaking beauty, we can be certain that our efforts will help keep it that way, thanks to the National Park Service.

Essential Details:

- ***Opening Hours and Admission Costs****: The Grand Canyon is open 24 hours a day, year-round, although some areas are seasonal. The South Rim is accessible all year, while the North Rim is generally open from mid-May to mid-October. Entrance fees are $35 per vehicle, which provides access for seven days.*
- ***Recommended Hotels and Camping****: Accommodation options range from luxurious to rustic. Near the South Rim, El Tovar Hotel offers historic charm with rooms starting around $200 per night. For those seeking a closer connection to nature,*

Mather Campground on the South Rim provides well-maintained sites with advance reservations recommended, starting at $18 per night.

- **Recommended Restaurants**: *Dining in the park gives you several options. El Tovar Dining Room offers fine dining with a view of the canyon. For a more casual meal, Bright Angel Restaurant serves hearty, comforting dishes perfect after a day of hiking.*

- **Best Time of Year and Visit Duration**: *The best times to visit are during the spring and fall to avoid the summer crowds and intense heat. Most visitors find that two to three days allow enough time to explore the main viewpoints and trails comfortably.*

- **Must-Do Experiences**: *Don't miss a sunrise or sunset from Hopi Point on the South Rim, where the views are particularly stunning. Also, consider booking a helicopter tour for a breathtaking aerial perspective of the canyon. For the adventurous, a hike down to the Colorado River or a rafting trip on it offers an unforgettable experience blending adventure with unique canyon views.*

1.2: Antelope Canyon: A Sculpture of Light and Stone

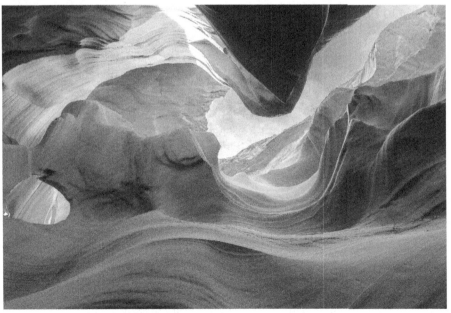

Unveiling Antelope Canyon

Antelope Canyon is a breathtaking example of natural beauty and artistic skill, hidden away in the Navajo Nation. Naturalists have described this stunning slot canyon as looking like an abstract sculpture due to its winding passages and sloping stone walls. Here, the visual spectacle is always evolving as the interplay of light and shadow creates a kaleidoscope of hues.

A Geological Phenomenon

Through millions of years of continuous wind and water erosion, Navajo sandstone formed the channels that now make up Antelope Canyon. Every nook and cranny here reveals something new about the Earth's ever-changing past, making this geological wonder the stuff of geologists' fantasies. Upper Antelope Canyon, also known as "The Crack," and Lower Antelope Canyon, also known as "The Corkscrew," are two separate parts of the canyon that provide different viewpoints and photo ops.

Photographic and Cultural Icon

Antelope Canyon is a paradise for photographers and ecotourists due to its internationally renowned picturesque qualities. The most dramatic shots are taken when sunlight streams through the tiny holes and lights up the sand below. In addition to its scenic value, the canyon is highly esteemed by the Navajo people for the sacredness it represents in relation to the strength and perseverance of the Earth.

Exploring the Canyon

Only on guided excursions conducted by native Navajo people is it possible to fully immerse oneself in the Antelope Canyon experience. Both the preservation of the site and the enrichment of the visit with cultural anecdotes and historical insights are achieved through these visits. A stroll around the canyon becomes an adventure across time and space as each guide's story enhances the scenic beauty.

Essential Details:

- ***Opening Hours and Admission Costs:*** *Antelope Canyon is accessible only through guided tours, which are available generally from 8:00 AM to 5:00 PM daily. The cost for tours varies, typically ranging from $40 to $90 per person depending on the time of day and the specific section of the canyon you choose to visit (Upper or Lower Antelope Canyon).*

- **Recommended Hotels and Camping:** *Stay nearby in Page, Arizona, where accommodations suit all budgets. The Courtyard by Marriott offers comfortable rooms with modern amenities starting around $150 per night. For those who prefer to camp, the Page Lake Powell Campground provides facilities close to nature with tent sites available from about $30 per night.*

- **Recommended Restaurants:** *Indulge in local flavors at Big John's Texas BBQ in Page, known for its smoked meats and casual atmosphere. Another great option is the Blue Buddha Sushi Lounge for those craving something lighter and different.*

- **Best Time of Year and Visit Duration:** *The best times to visit are during spring and fall to avoid the extreme heat and larger crowds of summer. The lighting is particularly spectacular for photography between late morning and early afternoon when the sun is high. Most visitors find that a half-day tour (2-3 hours) is sufficient to experience the canyon's beauty, though photography enthusiasts may wish to book multiple tours at different times of the day.*

- **Must-Do Experiences:** *Ensure your tour includes a visit during times when sunlight penetrates deep into the canyon, casting beams that illuminate the sandstone walls in breathtaking hues. The photographic tours are highly recommended, as they are tailored to capturing the play of light within the canyons.*

Discovering Havasu Falls

Havasu Falls, tucked away in the Grand Canyon, is a hidden treasure that few people know about. The red canyon walls provide a dramatic contrast to the breathtaking blue-green waters of this waterfall, creating an almost surreal paradise. Havasu Falls is a spectacular destination, but getting there is just as exciting and peaceful.

The Journey to the Falls

Starting from Hualapai Hilltop, the ten-mile hike descends into Havasupai Canyon after winding over harsh desert terrain. As you make your way up the steep trail, you'll be rewarded with beautiful panoramas until you reach the base of the falls. As they make their way along the trail, hikers can be serenaded by the soothing sound of running water.

The Lure of Turquoise Waters

The Havasu Falls cascades down a 100-foot cliff and into a huge, tranquil lake below. In addition to its breathtaking beauty, this natural wonder is famous for the healing properties of its mineral-rich waters. If you swim in the pool under the falls while surrounded by verdant vegetation, you will feel as if you have escaped to a tropical paradise, far from the scorching desert sun.

Cultural Significance

As the land's custodians, the Havasupai people hold Havasu Falls in the highest regard. Here, the water symbolizes rebirth and life, and the location represents the close bond between the people and their traditional homeland. Tourists are treated like royalty and given the chance to immerse themselves in the tribe's rich history and culture, which makes the experience all the more meaningful.

Essential Details:

- **Opening Hours and Admission Costs**: *Havasu Falls is accessible all year, but visiting requires a permit from the Havasupai Tribe. The tribe releases permits in February for the entire year, and they often sell out quickly. Permits include all necessary fees for camping, entrance, and environmental care, typically costing around $375-450 per person for a three-night stay.*

- **Recommended Hotels and Camping**: *While there are no hotels directly at Havasu Falls, the nearby village of Supai offers the Havasupai Lodge, with rooms starting around $440 per night, suitable for those looking for a more comfortable stay before beginning their hike to the falls. Most visitors choose to camp at the designated campground near Havasu Falls, which is included in the permit price.*

- **Recommended Restaurants**: *Dining options are limited in this remote area. Visitors generally need to bring their own food for camping. However, there is a small café in Supai Village where you can purchase simple meals and snacks.*

- **Best Time of Year and Visit Duration**: *The best time to visit Havasu Falls is during the spring (March to May) and fall (September to November) when the weather is cooler and more conducive to hiking. A stay of three to four days is ideal, allowing ample time to explore the falls, hike additional trails, and fully enjoy the natural beauty of the area.*

- **Must-Do Experiences**: *Beyond simply viewing the stunning falls, be sure to hike to Mooney Falls and Beaver Falls, located further downstream. These additional falls offer more secluded swimming areas and spectacular photo opportunities. Also, consider a night of stargazing; the clear skies and lack of light pollution make for an incredible celestial display.*

1.4: Petrified Forest National Park: A Journey Through Time

Exploring Ancient Landscapes

You will feel like you've stepped into another time when you visit Petrified Forest National Park. In this location, surrounded by vividly colored deserts and expansive blue skies, the fossilized remains of long-gone trees tell a tale that dates back millions of years. In addition to being a visual feast, this extraordinary terrain provides a window into the Earth's primordial life.

The Painted Desert's Palette

The trip starts out in the far from desolate Painted Desert. Variegated shades of rich reds, oranges, and purples that change as the sun moves across the sky are what make this part of the park famous for its spectacular hues. Seeing the Earth's surface painted in hues that appear to originate from another planet is a bizarre and otherworldly experience.

A Forest Frozen in Time

The petrified wood, which is the park's namesake, awaits you as you continue on your journey. Permineralization, an intriguing process that took place more than 225 million years ago, transformed these old plants into stone. Their crystalline surfaces reflect a variety of hues as they shine beneath the sun. You feel as though you are touching a fragment of Earth's long history as you stroll amid these natural artworks.

The Heart of the Park: The Rainbow Forest

The Rainbow Forest is located in the very center of the Petrified Forest. It has the greatest concentration of petrified wood, giving the impression that you are hiking through a forest that has been frozen in time. The scene is quite surreal—the logs that once supported life now rest as exquisite stone sculptures, each one bearing a story of the verdant vegetation that formerly thrived in this very spot.

Cultural Crossroads

In addition to being a paradise for those interested in the natural world, this park is rich in human history. The Petrified Forest is a cultural crossroads, displaying the connections between people and this magical terrain through the millennia, from historic structures from the park's early days as a tourist attraction to prehistoric petroglyphs engraved into rock faces by early residents.

Essential Details:

- **Opening Hours and Admission Costs**: *The park is open daily from 7:00 AM to 7:00 PM during the summer months and 8:00 AM to 5:00 PM during the winter months. Admission is $25 per vehicle, which grants you access for seven days, allowing plenty of time to explore all that the park has to offer.*

- **Recommended Hotels and Camping**: *For those looking to stay overnight, the nearby town of Holbrook offers several lodging options. Consider the Globetrotter Lodge, known for its clean, retro-style rooms and welcoming atmosphere, with prices starting around $100 per night. For camping enthusiasts, the Crystal Forest Campground located within the park offers a chance to sleep among the ancient stones, with no fee or reservations required.*

- **Recommended Restaurants**: *After a day of exploring, you can enjoy a meal at Mesa Italiana Restaurant in Holbrook, which offers hearty Italian fare perfect for refueling. For a quicker, diner-style meal, head to Tom & Suzie's Diner, known for its friendly service and classic American breakfasts and burgers.*

- **Best Time of Year and Visit Duration**: *Spring and fall are the best times to visit the Petrified Forest National Park, offering mild weather and the vibrant colors of changing seasons. Most visitors find that one to two days are sufficient to hike several trails, visit the Rainbow Forest Museum, and drive through the park's scenic roads.*

- **Must-Do Experiences**: *Don't miss the opportunity to walk the Giant Logs Trail near the Rainbow Forest Museum, where some of the park's largest and most colorful petrified logs are found. Also, the Blue Mesa area with its badlands of bluish bentonite clay offers not only fantastic photo opportunities but also a surreal hiking experience.*

1.5: Monument Valley: Land of Timeless Majesty

Stepping into the Scene

Located on the border between Arizona and Utah, Monument Valley is a breathtaking example of nature's craftsmanship. Spectacular red spires and expansive sandy plains reach for the heavens here, transporting you to a Mars-like landscape. The holy land of the Navajo people, this iconic landscape has been captured in innumerable images and films, and it symbolizes the classic American West.

Cinematic Backdrop

The experience of entering Monument Valley is like to entering a massive film set. When you see the valley's Mittens and Merrick Butte on the horizon in a film like "Forrest Gump" or a classic John Ford Western, you might immediately know the setting. The Navajo people have been influenced by the rough beauty of the West for many years, and this location brings together the cinematic history of the Wild West with that beauty.

The Majesty of the Mittens

Famous for their outstretched shadows that dance across the valley floor as the sun rises and sets, the East and West Mittens stand like hands reaching upwards in this park. The visitor center or the scenic drive provide excellent vantage points from which to photograph these formations, which, when lit up, reveal the desert's ever-changing grandeur.

Cultural Riches

In addition to its breathtaking scenery, Monument Valley is rich in Navajo history and culture. Navajo tour guides are a great way to learn about the culture, myths, and modern-day Navajo people. In order to gain a more profound appreciation for this hallowed setting, these trips may lead you to lesser-known locations, such as rock art sites, ancient ruins, and arches.

Essential Details:

- ***Opening Hours and Admission Costs****: Monument Valley Navajo Tribal Park is open year-round, though hours vary by season. Generally, the visitor center operates from 6 AM to 8 PM during peak season (May to Sept) and 8 AM to 5 PM in the off-season (Oct to Apr). The entrance fee is $20 per vehicle, which includes up to four people.*

- ***Recommended Hotels and Camping****: For a memorable stay, consider The View Hotel, strategically positioned to offer spectacular views of the famous mittens right from your room. Room rates start at about $95 per night. For those preferring to camp, The View Campground offers facilities for both RVs and tents, with rates starting at $30 per night for a basic tent site.*

- ***Recommended Restaurants****: Dine at The View Restaurant, located within the hotel, offering a menu that includes both Navajo-inspired dishes and more familiar American options, all while you enjoy the sweeping views of the valley. For a quick snack or a casual meal, Goulding's Stagecoach Dining Room is another great option nearby, serving up hearty Southwestern fare.*

- ***Best Time of Year and Visit Duration****: The best times to visit are during the spring and fall when temperatures are milder and the lighting is ideal for photography. Most visitors find that one to two days are sufficient to take in the major scenic points and perhaps join a guided tour.*

- ***Must-Do Experiences****: Don't miss a guided tour, whether self-driven or led by a Navajo guide, which will take you closer to famous formations like the East and West Mittens, John Ford's Point, and the Totem Pole. Sunrise and sunset tours are particularly magical, offering a play of colors that brings the landscape to life in a way that's truly spectacular.*

1.6: Saguaro National Park: A Sentinel of the Desert

Welcoming the Giants

The breathtaking scenery of Saguaro National Park is here to honor the famous saguaro cactus. This tall plant, unique to the Sonoran Desert, watches over a strange and unpredictable place with an air of stoicism. You can get a different feel for the thriving desert culture of southern Arizona by exploring the two separate areas here: the Tucson Mountain District (West) and the Rincon Mountain District (East).

The Land of the Saguaros

Standing as old sentinels of the desert, the saguaros grab everyone's attention the moment they enter the park. Some of them are more than 40 feet tall. The surrounding environment relies on these cacti for food and shelter, therefore they're more than just plants. As the sun beats down on the desert in late spring and early summer, their white blossoms turn the landscape into a verdant oasis.

Diverse Desert Life

The saguaro cacti are just one part of Saguaro National Park. The park is teeming with wildlife, from majestic golden eagles to nocturnal coyotes and vibrant wildflowers. Nature enthusiasts, photographers, and hikers abound at this popular destination because to the diverse landscape it offers, which includes rocky hills, desert flats, and scarce woodlands. The area provides a glimpse of the Sonoran Desert's biodiversity.

Trails and Tales

Exploring Saguaro National Park on foot is like walking through a verdant storybook. Hikes up Wasson Peak, from which one can see across the desert floor to the busy city of Tucson, are among the more strenuous trails available, while more leisurely options include the Valley View Overlook Trail. Views of this dry but unexpectedly vibrant terrain can be had from any of the paths.

Essential Details:

- *Opening Hours and Admission Costs: Saguaro National Park is open 24 hours a day, 365 days a year. The Rincon Mountain District (East) and Tucson Mountain District (West) visitor centers are open daily from 9:00 AM to 5:00 PM, except on Christmas Day. The entrance fee is $25 per vehicle, which covers all passengers and is valid for 7 days.*

- *Recommended Hotels and Camping: For those looking to stay nearby, the Tanque Verde Ranch offers comfortable lodging with a touch of luxury and rooms starting at about $200 per night. For camping enthusiasts, the Gilbert Ray Campground located in the Tucson Mountain District provides well-equipped sites with beautiful desert views, with rates around $20 per night for a standard site.*

- *Recommended Restaurants: After a day of hiking, you can enjoy a meal at the Saguaro Corners Restaurant, which offers delicious southwestern dishes in a relaxed setting. Another great option is the Coyote Pause Café, offering hearty, home-cooked meals perfect for refueling after exploring.*

- *Best Time of Year and Visit Duration: The best times to visit the park are during the cooler months from October to April when the desert heat is more tolerable. Most visitors find that one to two days are sufficient to explore the highlights of both the east and west districts of the park.*

- *Must-Do Experiences: Be sure not to miss the scenic drives like the Cactus Forest Loop in the East District and the Bajada Loop Drive in the West District, which offer stunning views and numerous photo opportunities. Hiking the trails, such as the Hugh Norris Trail or the Mica View Trail, provides close encounters with the diverse flora and fauna. Also, consider joining a ranger-led program to learn more about the desert ecosystem and the cultural history of the area.*

1.7: Organ Pipe Cactus National Monument: A Desert Refuge

Exploring the Unique Landscape

Organ Pipe Cactus National Monument in southern Arizona's Sonoran Desert is a verdant showcase of the abundant flora and fauna that survive in the harsh climate. Organ pipe cactus is the inspiration for the name of this uncommon and lovely species, which takes pride in its place among many other desert plants and animals in an exceptionally unspoiled area of the American desert.

A Symphony of Stone and Sand

The remarkable array of desert flora, including the distinctive organ pipe cactus, create a dramatic canvas in the monument's terrain. Hikers can expect to see a wide variety of life forms as they venture through the scenic roadways and challenging backcountry routes, from towering saguaros to fragile wildflowers.

The Night Blooms

An absolutely must-see is the night-blooming organ pipe cactus. The moonlight brings these plants to life as the smaller long-nosed bats silently pollinate the white flowers, making them sparkle in the dark. This extraordinary occurrence highlights the special ecological importance of this region and serves as a poignant reminder of the complex web of relationships present in the desert.

Cultural Tapestry

Numerous human activities, including those of the ancient Hohokam people, the Spanish, and later American prospectors, have left their imprints on this monument. The park's cultural sites provide light on the ways in which indigenous peoples have shaped and adapted to this desert environment over the course of thousands of years.

Essential Details:

- ***Opening Hours and Admission Costs****: The monument is open 24 hours a day, year-round, but the Kris Eggle Visitor Center operates from 8:00 AM to 5:00 PM daily, except on December 25. Entrance fees are $25 per vehicle, which covers all passengers for seven days, providing ample time to explore the vast landscape.*

- **Recommended Hotels and Camping**: *For those looking to stay overnight, the Sonoran Desert Inn in Ajo offers a comfortable stay with a blend of history and modern amenities, with rooms starting around $100 per night. Within the monument, the Twin Peaks Campground offers camping sites suitable for both tents and RVs, with facilities available for around $20 per night.*
- **Recommended Restaurants**: *In nearby Ajo, try the 100 Estrella Restaurant, known for its delicious Sonoran-style Mexican dishes. Another great spot is Marcela's Café, offering a range of hearty and comforting meals ideal after a day of hiking.*
- **Best Time of Year and Visit Duration**: *The best times to visit are from November to March when temperatures are cooler and more comfortable for exploring. Most visitors find that two to three days are sufficient to enjoy a comprehensive tour of the monument, including scenic drives and key hikes.*
- **Must-Do Experiences**: *Don't miss the scenic Ajo Mountain Drive, a 21-mile loop that offers breathtaking views and access to several short trails. Be sure to join a ranger-led program to learn more about the area's natural history and the fascinating cultural heritage of the Tohono O'odham Nation. Also, night-time stargazing is a must-do, with the monument's clear skies offering spectacular views of the Milky Way.*

1.8: Walnut Canyon National Monument: Echoes of Ancient Dwellings

Stepping Back in Time

Walnut Canyon National Monument, located to the east of Flagstaff, provides an intriguing window into the culture of the long-vanished inhabitants of this high desert oasis. As you meander through the canyon, you'll cross paths with the Sinagua, a tribe who perfected the skill of coexisting with the harsh desert climate.

The Canyon's Ancient Architecture

The cliff houses, skillfully constructed beneath limestone outcrops, are Walnut Canyon's most eye-catching landmarks. Made from the granite that protects them, these structures are incredibly well-preserved and narrate a tale of resourcefulness and perseverance. As you wander around, try to put yourself in the shoes of a family that lived here 700 years ago, flourishing in this spectacular setting by cultivating crops on the rim, hunting animals, and gathering medicinal and edible wild herbs.

A Hiker's Haven

Walnut Canyon is a hiking lover's dream as much as it is a historical site. On the moderately difficult Island Trail, you'll go straight past twenty-five cliff house rooms. Those seeking a more leisurely stroll can enjoy stunning vistas of the canyon and its environs from the Rim Trail, which also has informative exhibits detailing the cultural and environmental history of the region.

Echoes of the Past

You can almost hear the echoes of bygone activities as you stroll down Walnut Canyon, such as children playing, craftspeople at work, and families getting together. An ever-increasing sense of the Sinagua's adaptability and perseverance is left behind with each new detail about their everyday existence, from the food they consumed to the tools they made.

Essential Details:

- ***Opening Hours and Admission Costs****: Walnut Canyon is open from 9:00 AM to 4:30 PM daily, except on December 25. Admission is $15 per adult, which grants access for seven days. Children under 15 enter for free.*
- ***Recommended Hotels and Camping****: For comfortable lodging, consider staying in Flagstaff, just a short drive from the monument. The Little America Hotel offers luxurious accommodations with rooms starting at about $130 per night. For a closer-to-nature experience, the Bonito Campground near the monument provides excellent facilities during the summer months, with rates around $18 per night.*
- ***Recommended Restaurants****: Enjoy a meal at the Crown Railroad Cafe in Flagstaff, known for its quirky train-themed decor and hearty American classics. Alternatively, the Historic Downtown area offers a variety of dining options, including Brix Restaurant and Wine Bar for a more upscale dining experience.*
- ***Best Time of Year and Visit Duration****: Spring and fall are ideal for visiting, with comfortable temperatures and vibrant natural colors. Most visitors spend about half a day exploring the*

trails and viewing the cliff dwellings, though you could easily extend your visit with more hiking and exploration.

- **Must-Do Experiences**: *Don't miss the Island Trail, a moderate one-mile loop that descends into the canyon, giving you an up-close view of the ancient Sinagua cliff dwellings. For a less strenuous visit, the Rim Trail offers breathtaking views of the canyon and the surrounding landscapes with minimal walking required.*

1.9: Tonto National Monument – Preserving Salado Heritage

A Window to the Ancient World

Tonto National Monument, in Arizona's mountainous Tonto Basin, provides a unique window into the culture of the Salado people, who lived and flourished 700 years ago in Arizona's dry desert. The two cliff homes preserved at this national monument are living examples of human creativity and perseverance; they also give tourists a glimpse into the Salado people's rich cultural heritage.

Echoes of the Salado

Tourists can marvel at the intricate Salado architecture and artifacts left behind at Tonto National Monument's cliff homes, which have been astonishingly well-preserved. A short climb brings you to the Lower Cliff Dwelling, where the Salado people's profound awareness of their surroundings is on display in rooms constructed from a mix of cultural and natural materials. Those interested in learning more about the intricacies of their culture can do so on guided tours to the Upper Cliff Dwelling.

Immersive Experiences

Tonto National Monument is a place that transports visitors to a bygone era. In addition to breathtaking panoramas, the location also hosts educational programs that shed light on the Salado's creative expressions, agricultural practices, and methods of surviving in harsh environments. People of all ages can learn about the Salado's history through these programs, which are generally guided by well-informed park rangers.

A Sanctuary for Nature and History

The monument area is a sanctuary for native plants and animals, and it is encircled by the stunning Tonto National Forest, making it an ideal location for birdwatchers and ecotourists. A tranquil yet illuminating experience awaits anyone who go along its pathways, thanks to the harmonious interplay of history and natural beauty.

Essential Details:

- ***Opening Hours and Admission Costs***: *Tonto National Monument is open from 8:00 AM to 5:00 PM daily, except for major holidays. Admission is $10 per person, granting access to both the Lower and Upper Cliff Dwellings.*
- ***Recommended Hotels and Camping***: *Nearby Roosevelt Lake offers the Cholla Campground with facilities suitable for both tents and RVs, with rates starting at about $20 per night. For hotel accommodations, consider staying at the Apache Lake Resort, with room rates starting around $100 per night, offering rustic comfort and stunning lake views.*
- ***Recommended Restaurants***: *For dining, visit the nearby Butcher Hook Restaurant, known for its hearty meals and local charm, providing a taste of Arizona's rustic cuisine.*
- ***Best Time of Year to Visit***: *The best times to visit are during the cooler months from October to April, when the weather is ideal for hiking and exploring the outdoors.*
- ***Duration of Visit***: *A full day is recommended to explore the monument thoroughly, including time for guided tours and independent exploration.*
- ***Must-Do Experiences***: *Be sure not to miss a ranger-led tour to the Upper Cliff Dwelling, which provides additional historical context and spectacular views of the Tonto Basin. Also, take time to participate in one of the educational programs about Salado pottery or textile making.*

1.10: Montezuma Castle National Monument – Preserving Pueblo Heritage

Ancestral Puebloan Masterpiece

Located in Arizona's picturesque Verde Valley, the breathtaking Montezuma Castle National Monument stands as a monument to the Sinagua people's resourcefulness and perseverance in the face of the hostile desert environment. This five-story cliff residence provides a glimpse into the lives of an ancient civilization that had very sophisticated architectural abilities for their period. It is built into a limestone recess far above the earth.

Exploring the Sinagua Legacy

Montezuma Castle is one of the most impressive cliff houses in North America, and it welcomes guests who come to marvel at it. Built more than 800 years ago, this architectural marvel is also a spiritual location with a tale to tell about community, connection to the land, and survival. The adjacent Montezuma Well, a limestone sinkhole, is another example of the Sinagua's resourcefulness and adaptability; they grew vegetables in this unusual environment to support their community.

A Cultural Journey

As you meander around the paths surrounding Montezuma Castle, you'll pass serene Beaver Creek and verdant sycamore forests. Educational displays on the Sinagua people, their everyday lives, and the local environment may be found along each walk. Hiking these paths is more than just taking in some scenery; it's like diving headfirst into a rich history.

Conservation and Education

In addition to serving as a historical site, Montezuma Castle is a museum and educational institution. The Sinagua people's rich history is brought to life through the monument's visitor center's numerous displays and interactive exhibits. Visitors can learn more about this ancient civilization and the preservation efforts at this remarkable site through talks and guided tours given by rangers and volunteers.

Essential Details:

- **Opening Hours and Admission Costs**: *Montezuma Castle is open daily from 8:00 AM to 5:00 PM, except for Christmas Day. Admission is $10 per person, valid for seven days and includes entry to Montezuma Well.*
- **Recommended Hotels and Camping**: *Stay at the Beaver Creek Inn, located just a short drive from the monument, with rooms averaging $120 per night. For camping enthusiasts, the Rancho Verde RV Park offers a peaceful setting with rates starting at $35 per night.*
- **Recommended Restaurants**: *For a taste of local cuisine, visit the Verde Brewing Company, which offers craft beers and hearty meals. Nikki's Grill is another great spot for comfort food in a cozy setting.*
- **Best Time of Year to Visit**: *The ideal times to visit are during the spring and fall when temperatures are mild and the natural scenery is at its most vibrant.*
- **Duration of Visit**: *Plan to spend at least half a day at the monument to fully appreciate the site and its surroundings.*
- **Must-Do Experiences**: *Don't miss the ranger-led tour of Montezuma Castle to gain deeper insights into the Sinagua culture and the architectural significance of the cliff dwellings. Be sure to also visit Montezuma Well to see the ancient irrigation systems still visible today.*

1.11: Wupatki National Monument – Legacy of the Ancestral Puebloans

Rediscovering Ancient Civilizations

Ancestral Puebloans once flourished in this austere, hypnotic region; Wupatki National Monument in northern Arizona provides a fascinating look into their lives. Located in a desert setting, the monument's remarkably well-preserved ruins provide a moving window into a sophisticated culture that thrived more than nine centuries ago.

Exploring the Ruins

As evidence of the ancient people' architectural skill and inventiveness, Wupatki is littered with the remnants of red sandstone buildings. Among the many pueblos that are open to the public is the magnificent Wupatki Pueblo, which was formerly the biggest structure for kilometers and an important cultural and economic hub. By following the paths that wind around the monument, visitors may get a closer look at these old homes and feel more connected to the past.

Cultural Crossroads

Wupatki was more than a house; it brought people of all backgrounds together. Interactions between the Sinagua, Cohonina, and Kayenta Anasazi groups are visible in the artifacts and building styles of this site. The site's renowned ball court and community room showcase the cultural richness of the region by suggesting a complex social structure with communal and ceremonial significance.

A Desert Surrounded by Natural Beauty

Spectacular views are offered by the ancient ruins set against the vivid landscape, which in turn offers stunning views of the Painted Desert and the San Francisco Peaks. Natural beauty complements the area's historical wealth, creating a tranquil yet stark atmosphere that heightens tourists' sense of discovery.

Essential Details:

- ***Opening Hours and Admission Costs****: Wupatki National Monument is open daily from sunrise to sunset. The Visitor Center is open from 9:00 AM to 5:00 PM. Admission is $25 per vehicle,* which includes entry to both Wupatki and Sunset Crater Volcano National Monuments.

- **Recommended Hotels and Camping**: For those wishing to stay nearby, the Little America Hotel in Flagstaff offers comfortable accommodations with prices starting at about $130 per night. For camping enthusiasts, Bonito Campground is located just outside Sunset Crater Volcano National Monument, offering sites at $26 per night.
- **Recommended Restaurants**: Enjoy local flavors at Satchmo's in Flagstaff, known for its BBQ and Cajun dishes, or try Fat Olives for authentic Italian cuisine.
- **Best Time of Year to Visit**: The best times to visit are during the spring and fall when the weather is milder and the natural scenery is at its most vibrant.
- **Duration of Visit**: Plan to spend at least a full day exploring the monument to fully appreciate the historical sites and surrounding landscapes.
- **Must-Do Experiences**: Don't miss the guided tours offered by rangers, which provide insightful narratives about the lives of the Ancestral Puebloans. Also, ensure to visit the nearby Sunset Crater Volcano National Monument for a complete understanding of the geological and cultural history of the area.

1.12: Canyon de Chelly National Monument – Echoes of Ancestral Spirits

A Sacred Landscape

Located in northeastern Arizona, Canyon de Chelly National Monument is a powerful symbol of the Navajo people's culture and resiliency. The canyon is both a breathtaking natural formation and a historical repository for Native Americans, thanks to its centuries-old cliff houses, ancient rock art, and soaring sandstone cliffs.

Traces of the Past

As you hike the paths or drive along the scenic roads, you are following in the footsteps of the Navajo and Ancestral Puebloans, who have inhabited this area for thousands of years. Pictographs and petroglyphs adorn the canyon walls, portraying the indigenous people's everyday lives, spiritual practices, and deep connections to the land.

Vibrant Culture and Traditions

Even now, the Navajo people still consider Canyon de Chelly an important cultural site. Being fully on Navajo Tribal Trust Land—which includes a residential village and farmland—makes it unique among U.S. national monuments. Through guided tours given by Navajo guides, visitors to the monument can appreciate not only the breathtaking natural beauty but also the lasting legacy of the Navajo culture, which gives the monument a distinct viewpoint.

Natural Majesty

Spider Rock is a holy spire to the Navajo people, and the monument's topography showcases a breathtaking variety of sceneries, from the towering cliffs to the verdant canyon floors, drained by the Chinle and Tsaile streams. The varied landscapes shown by the many trails and vantage points are as varied as the seasons and the time of day.

Essential Details:

- ***Opening Hours and Admission Costs****: Canyon de Chelly is open year-round, and there is no fee to enter the park. However, access to the canyon floor is restricted and only possible with a Navajo guide except for the White House Ruin Trail.*
- ***Recommended Hotels and Camping****: Stay at the Thunderbird Lodge located just inside the park, with rooms averaging $120 per night. For camping, Cottonwood*

Campground offers basic facilities free of charge on a first-come, first-served basis.

- **Recommended Restaurants**: *Try the Junction Restaurant in Chinle, known for its blend of traditional Navajo dishes and American classics.*
- **Best Time of Year to Visit**: *Spring (April to June) and fall (September to November) offer pleasant weather, making it ideal for exploring the canyon.*
- **Duration of Visit**: *Allocate at least two days to fully explore the various overlooks, take part in a guided tour, and possibly hike the White House Ruin Trail.*
- **Must-Do Experiences**: *Book a Jeep tour with a Navajo guide to explore the canyon floor—a unique opportunity to learn about the Navajo culture firsthand. Don't miss the chance to view Spider Rock at sunset, when the spire glows brilliantly as the sun descends.*

1.13: Navajo National Monument – A Window into Ancestral Puebloan Life

Preserving Ancient Histories

Navajo National Monument, in the vast landscapes of northern Arizona, provides a deep look into the Ancestral Puebloans' way of life. Several impressive cliff homes, such as those at Betatakin and Keet Seel, are located within this tranquil monument. They silently guard the ancient peoples' illustrious past.

Cliff Dwellings and Cultural Echoes

As a cultural link between the old and the new, Navajo National Monument is much more than a historical landmark. Immerse yourself in the rich history, spiritual practices, and social structure of the Ancestral Puebloans as you go on guided tours of their cliff houses, which are set in the picturesque Tsegi Canyon system.

Trail Through Time

Guests can enjoy breathtaking vistas and educational opportunities along the monument's several routes. With interpretative panels detailing the local flora, animals, and history, the Sandal Trail is a pleasant paved route that leads to a lookout point above the Betatakin ruins. Adventurers who book in advance can go on a guided hike into Keet Seel, where they can see one of the biggest and best-preserved cliff houses up close.

Integrating Nature and Culture

Natural history and Ancestral Puebloan culture are on display at the monument's visitor center. In addition to learning about the old Navajo culture, visitors can also get an understanding of the modern Navajo way of life, which helps to bridge the gap between the two groups.

Essential Details:

- ***Opening Hours and Admission Costs****: Navajo National Monument is open year-round with free admission. Guided tours to the cliff dwellings are available from Memorial Day to Labor Day and require prior reservations.*
- ***Recommended Hotels and Camping****: The monument offers two free campgrounds, Sunset View and Canyon View, which operate on a first-come, first-served basis. For hotel accommodations, consider staying in Kayenta, about 20 miles away, where the Kayenta Monument Valley Inn offers rooms starting at $110 per night.*
- ***Recommended Restaurants****: The Blue Coffee Pot in Kayenta serves up hearty, locally-inspired meals, perfect after a day of exploring.*
- ***Best Time of Year to Visit****: The best time to visit is during the spring and fall when temperatures are moderate and the guided tours are less crowded.*
- ***Duration of Visit****: Plan at least a two-day visit to fully experience the guided tours and self-guided trails.*
- ***Must-Do Experiences****: Join a ranger-led tour to Betatakin, which offers an in-depth look at the incredible cliff dwellings and the natural environment that supported ancient life here. Don't miss the evening programs at the campground amphitheater, where rangers share stories of the stars, local wildlife, and the ancient peoples who once called this place home.*

1.14: Sunset Crater Volcano – A Monument to Nature's Power

A Landscape Sculpted by Fire

Located north of Flagstaff, Sunset Crater Volcano National Monument provides an awe-inspiring glimpse into the destructive force of volcanic eruptions and their far-reaching effects on the local environment. Geologists, historians, and nature lovers are enchanted by the lava flows and cinder cones left behind by Sunset Crater's last eruption, which occurred approximately 900 years ago. The volcano is the youngest in a series of volcanic features on the Colorado Plateau.

The Birth of a Volcano

Sunset Crater Volcano is a great place to study geological processes and ecological succession because of the way the eruption changed the local climate and landscape. The crimson rim of the crater, formed by oxidized cinders, provides breathtaking scenery and a stark illustration of the destructive and creative power of nature.

Trails Through Time

Sunset Crater is home to numerous paths that meander among cinder fields and lava flows. You can walk over solidified lava and get up close to the volcanic features on the accessible one-mile Lava Flow Trail. With sweeping vistas of the expansive Bonito Lava Flow and the San Francisco Peaks, the Cinder Hills Overlook Trail provides a more strenuous ascent for those seeking a more demanding adventure.

Life Amidst the Ashes

Life persists in Sunset Crater despite the extreme volcanic conditions. The monument showcases the adaptability and flourishing of plants and fauna in a healing landscape, making it a study in resilience. Ponderosa pines, aspen forests, and spring and summer blooming wildflowers dot the landscape surrounding the volcano's base, offering a striking contrast to the black volcanic rock.

Essential Details:

- ***Opening Hours and Admission Costs****: Sunset Crater Volcano National Monument is open year-round from sunrise to sunset. The entrance fee is $25 per vehicle, which also covers entry* to nearby *Wupatki National Monument and is valid for seven days.*

- **Recommended Hotels and Camping**: *The nearest accommodations are in Flagstaff, about 15 miles south. Little America Hotel offers a comfortable stay with prices starting around $130 per night. For camping enthusiasts, Bonito Campground is located just outside the monument and offers facilities for tents and RVs, with rates starting at $26 per night during its open season from May to October.*
- **Recommended Restaurants**: *Flagstaff has a variety of dining options. Beaver Street Brewery offers hearty meals perfect for refueling after a day of hiking, while Diablo Burger serves locally sourced gourmet burgers.*
- **Best Time of Year to Visit**: *The best times to visit are late spring and early fall when the weather is mild, and the natural scenery is at its most vibrant.*
- **Duration of Visit**: *Most visitors spend a full day at the monument to hike the trails and explore the visitor center's exhibits.*
- **Must-Do Experiences**: *Don't miss the interactive displays at the visitor center, which provide insights into the geological and ecological aspects of the area. Make sure to hike the Lava Flow Trail for a close-up view of the volcanic formations and the opportunity to walk through a lava tube.*

Chapter 2: Discovering Arizona's Cultural Heritage

2.1: Heard Museum

Celebrating Indigenous Art and Culture

Phoenix, Arizona's Heard Museum is a must-visit for anybody interested in Native American art and culture. This museum is renowned for its commitment to promoting American Indian art. It is more than just a repository of historical items; it is a thriving cultural center that highlights the art, history, and voices of Indigenous peoples.

A Window to Native Heritage

The Heard Museum features a vast collection of Native American artworks, ranging from modern fine art to traditional hand-woven Navajo textiles. Its interactive exhibits, such "HOME: Native People in the Southwest," take visitors on a journey into the culture, religion, and daily life of the indigenous peoples of the Southwest. Crafted from the Native American point of view, these exhibits provide a window into Native American history and culture as it exists now.

Interactive and Educational Experiences

The museum serves as a hub for educational programming that helps both locals and tourists appreciate the diverse Native American heritage. Native American artists will typically lead art workshops, cultural demonstrations, and live performances. Visitors are not only educated, but also brought closer to the Indigenous communities' genuine cultural manifestations through these encounters.

Festivals and Special Events

Numerous festivals and activities showcasing Native American culture are held at the Heard Museum all year round. Among these, the World Championship Hoop Dance Contest stands out for bringing together skilled dancers from all around North America. If you want to feel the energy of Indigenous cultures for yourself, you must attend these events, which honor Native American artwork.

Essential Details:

- *Opening Hours and Admission Costs: The museum is open from 9:30 AM to 5:00 PM, Monday to Saturday, and from 11:00 AM to 5:00 PM on Sundays. Admission is $20 for adults, with discounts available for students, children, and seniors.*
- *Recommended Hotels: Stay at the nearby Sheraton Phoenix Downtown for a comfortable visit, with rates starting around $150 per night.*
- *Recommended Restaurants: Enjoy modern Southwestern cuisine at the Fry Bread House, a local favorite just a short drive from the museum.*
- *Best Time to Visit: Visit during the cooler months from November to April for a pleasant experience. Plan to spend at least half a day exploring the museum's extensive exhibits.*
- *Must-Do Experiences: Do not miss the opportunity to attend a live cultural performance or a festival if your visit coincides with these events. They provide a deep insight into the traditions and artistry of Native American cultures.*

2.2: Taliesin West

Architectural Harmony with Nature

Located in Scottsdale, Arizona, in the desert foothills of the McDowell Mountains, Taliesin West is more than just a building site; it is a living manifestation of Frank Lloyd Wright's eco-friendly ideology. Built in 1937 as the famous architect's winter residence and studio, it is now a thriving hub for architectural ideas and practices.

A Living Laboratory

Wright incorporated the desert environment into the architecture of Taliesin West by utilizing natural materials that reflected the terrain. Built by locally sourced stone and desert sands, the buildings cleverly disappear into their natural surroundings. Taliesin West is a real-life example of Wright's organic architectural philosophy, with every turn designed to improve the interaction between the natural environment and the indoor areas.

Innovative Educational Hub

The Frank Lloyd Wright School of Architecture is located in Taliesin West, which is also a National Historic Landmark. Students live, work, and study the principles of Wright's designs here, carrying on his legacy of environmentally conscious architecture. Students are encouraged to think creatively and respond imaginatively to their environment in the hands-on learning environment.

Cultural and Artistic Events

An architectural and cultural gem, Taliesin West is a place of many uses. All through the year, it plays host to a wide range of community activities, seminars, and workshops that delve into different facets of architecture and design. Participating in these activities, which are frequently held in Wright's breathtakingly beautiful environments, is a great way to learn and be inspired.

Essential Details:

- ***Opening Hours and Admission Costs****: Taliesin West offers tours ranging from one to three hours long, available daily from 9:00 AM to 4:00 PM. Prices vary by tour type, generally starting around $35 per person.*
- ***Recommended Hotels****: For those looking to extend their stay, the Hyatt Regency Scottsdale Resort & Spa offers luxury accommodations with desert views, starting around $200 per night.*
- ***Recommended Restaurants****: Nearby, the Spiga Cucina Italiana offers exquisite Italian dishes perfect for a post-tour dinner. Another great option is the Mission, where modern Latin cuisine can be savored.*

- **Best Time of Year to Visit**: *The best time to visit is from October to April, when the weather is cooler and more comfortable for exploring.*
- **Duration of Visit**: *Plan to spend at least half a day at Taliesin West, including the time on your chosen tour and some additional time to soak in the surroundings.*
- **Must-Do Experiences**: *Don't miss the 'Insights Tour', a comprehensive tour that gives you an intimate look at Wright's living quarters and studios. Also, check for any special nighttime events or lectures that offer a unique way to experience the space and learn more about Wright's work.*

2.3: Arizona-Sonora Desert Museum

A Fusion of Zoo, Botanical Garden, and Art Gallery

Located outside of Tucson, the Arizona-Sonora Desert Museum is an unusual zoo, botanical park, and art gallery all rolled into one. Immerse yourself in the Sonoran Desert's life at this breathtaking outdoor museum spanning 98 acres. Beyond being a museum, it becomes an outdoor adventure of culture and nature along two miles of pathways that wind through different desert habitats.

Discover the Wonders of the Sonoran Desert

You may get up close and personal with native animals including Gila monsters, prairie dogs, and mountain lions at the museum's live animal exhibits. The botanical gardens, which display more than 1,200 species of local plants, are just as stunning as the incredible variety of live animals housed there. As you make your way along the trail, you'll learn more about the unique ways that plants and animals survive in this dry environment.

Engaging with Nature

At the Earth Sciences Center, one of the best parts of the museum, you may learn about local geology by going below in a limestone cavern. Raptor Free Flight is one of the museum's interactive experiences; it features native birds of prey performing stunning demonstrations low over the crowd with no barriers separating them from the spectators.

A Hub for Conservation and Education

The Sonoran Desert is both culturally and ecologically significant, and the museum's programs aim to teach guests about this fact. It's an area where conservation isn't only talked about; it's also done, with programs designed to preserve the region's history and environment.

- **Opening Hours and Admission Costs**: *The museum is open daily from 8:30 AM to 5:00 PM, with last admission at 4:15 PM. Admission is $23.95 for adults, with discounts available for seniors, military, and children.*
- **Recommended Hotels and Camping**: *Nearby, the Starr Pass Golf Suites offer a comfortable stay with desert vistas, starting around $120 per night. For a closer-to-nature experience, Gilbert Ray Campground offers excellent facilities and stunning desert scenery for about $20 per night.*
- **Recommended Restaurants**: *After your visit, enjoy some local flavors at Coyote Pause Café, offering a range of hearty Southwestern dishes. Another excellent choice is the Ocotillo Café within the museum itself, perfect for a quick lunch between exploring.*
- **Best Time of Year to Visit**: *The cooler months from October to April are ideal for visiting, allowing you to comfortably explore the outdoor exhibits.*
- **Duration of Visit**: *Plan to spend at least half a day at the museum, though you could easily fill a full day with all the exhibits and activities offered.*
- **Must-Do Experiences**: *Don't miss the Raptor Free Flight shows, particularly stunning during the cooler months when the birds are most active. Also, be sure to visit the Hummingbird Aviary, where these tiny birds dazzle visitors with their vibrant colors and aerial acrobatics.*

2.4: Old Tucson

Step into the Wild West

A gateway to the Old West, Old Tucson is more than simply an entertainment park. As you listen to the sounds of saloon music, the sound of boots on dusty streets, and the occasional shooting, you can almost feel the history pulsating in this breathtaking location near Tucson, Arizona, in the Sonoran Desert. Upon entering, you will be whisked away to a frontier town in the 1880s, replete with meticulously restored structures and an eerie, thrilling atmosphere.

A Living Movie Set

Although it was constructed in 1939 for the film "Arizona," Old Tucson has served as a setting for more than 300 films and TV series. Movie fans flock to this legendary site because it has played host to legendary western actors like John Wayne and Clint Eastwood. You never know when these icons' specters will pop up, waiting for their big moment, while you explore.

More Than Just a Set

On the other hand, Old Tucson has a lot more to offer than simply remake fever. Live stunt shows, musical performances, and gunfight reenactments bring the Old West to life in this exciting attraction. Everyone from history buffs to families may enjoy this immersive experience, where they can learn more about the American frontier through each structure, exhibit, and performance.

Essential Details:

- ***Opening Hours and Admission Costs****: Old Tucson is open from 10:00 AM to 6:00 PM daily. Entry fees are $19.95 for adults and $10.95 for children, which includes access to all live shows and demonstrations.*
- ***Recommended Hotels and Camping****: Nearby, the Starr Pass Golf Suites offer comfortable and scenic accommodations starting at around $120 per night. For those preferring to camp, Gilbert Ray Campground offers facilities close to nature at about $20 per night.*
- ***Recommended Restaurants****: Enjoy a meal at the Big Jake's BBQ at Old Tucson for a taste of authentic Western cuisine right in the setting of an old-time saloon. Outside the park, The Coyote Pause Café offers a casual dining experience with locally sourced ingredients.*
- ***Best Time of Year to Visit****: The cooler months from October to April provide the most pleasant experience. However, special holiday events like Halloween and Christmas offer unique thematic entertainment.*
- ***Duration of Visit****: Plan to spend at least a full day to take in all the shows and explore the numerous exhibits and attractions thoroughly.*
- ***Must-Do Experiences****: Don't miss the live stunt shows which are packed with action and authentic Wild West entertainment.*

Also, take the time to visit the miniature train exhibit and the carriages museum to see some original vehicles from the era.

2.5: Musical Instrument Museum

A Symphony of Global Culture

The Musical Instrument Museum (MIM) in Phoenix, Arizona, invites visitors to delve into the mesmerizing rhythms and melodies from throughout the globe. Among the world's most extensive collections of musical instruments, MIM provides an immersive experience that goes beyond the norm for museum visits by honoring music as a universal language.

A World of Music under One Roof

At MIM, you may see an incredible collection of over 8,000 instruments from almost 200 different countries. Careful curation ensures that each display does justice to the instrument while also elucidating its cultural background. As you get closer to each display, state-of-the-art headphones will begin playing the instruments' sounds, letting you experience their distinct tones while also seeing them played in their authentic contexts on dynamic video screens.

Interactive and Engaging Exhibits

Instead of just watching, MIM encourages you to get your hands dirty with the music-making process. Everyone can get their hands on, tune in to, and hear different instruments at the Experience Gallery. Learning to play an instrument, whether it's a harp or an African drum, is a great way to get your hands dirty and learn about the rich diversity of music.

Events and Performances

Musicians from all around the world perform at MIM's many events, including workshops, educational programs, and concerts. Attending one of these live performances is a great way to enrich your museum experience and learn more about the history and development of music.

Essential Details:

- ***Opening Hours and Admission Costs****: MIM is open daily from 9:00 AM to 5:00 PM. Admission is $20 for adults, with discounts available for teens, children, military, and seniors.*

- **Recommended Hotels**: *The nearby Marriott Phoenix Desert Ridge Resort & Spa offers luxurious accommodations with convenient access to the museum, with rates starting around $199 per night.*
- **Recommended Restaurants**: *For a dining experience that echoes the museum's global theme, try the nearby Tandoori Times for some of the best Indian cuisine in Phoenix. Another great option is the Wildflower Bread Company, known for its fresh, seasonal dishes.*
- **Best Time of Year to Visit**: *Phoenix is lovely during the fall and spring months when the weather is ideal for travel. However, indoor attractions like MIM are perfect year-round.*
- **Duration of Visit**: *Allocate at least half a day to fully experience the museum, though music enthusiasts may prefer a full day to thoroughly explore the exhibits and possibly catch a live performance.*
- **Must-Do Experiences**: *Be sure to check out the Artist Gallery, which features instruments played by legendary musicians such as John Lennon and Elvis Presley. Also, don't miss the opportunity to attend a live concert in MIM's acoustically superb theater.*

2.6: Arizona State Capitol Museum

Dive into Arizona's Rich History

Explore the rich history and cultural artifacts of Arizona at the Arizona State Capitol Museum in Phoenix. Housed in the historic Capitol building, this museum provides a vivid narrative of Arizona's history, beginning with its territorial days and continuing up to the present day. Each exhibit in the state capitol's vast hallways and former legislative chambers takes you on a journey through time, allowing you to better understand how this magnificent state came to be.

A Journey Through Time

From its Native American origins to its vital position in the American West, the museum's displays cover Arizona's rich history. Artifacts from Arizona's era as a U.S. territory and the USS Arizona Memorial, which honors the soldiers killed during the Pearl Harbor attack, are among the notable exhibitions. Moving from one room to another, the cultural and political history of Arizona is unveiled like a colorful tapestry.

Interactive and Educational Exhibits

The Arizona State Capitol Museum is not just a place to look and listen—it's a place to participate. Interactive displays, such as voting in a mock election or exploring a hands-on mining tunnel exhibit, engage visitors of all ages. These elements make the museum's narrative both accessible and compelling, especially for younger visitors.

Architectural Marvel

The building's fusion of neoclassical and Renaissance Revival styles makes it an architectural masterpiece in and of itself. Don't pass up the opportunity to see the Winged Victory monument and the stunning copper dome; they represent the resiliency and abundance of Arizona's natural resources.

Essential Details:

- ***Opening Hours and Admission Costs****: The museum is open Monday through Friday from 9:00 AM to 4:00 PM, with free admission for all visitors, making it an excellent option for families and history enthusiasts.*
- ***Recommended Hotels****: Stay at the nearby Hyatt Regency Phoenix for a comfortable visit, with room rates starting around $150 per night. This hotel offers easy access to downtown attractions, including the museum.*
- ***Recommended Restaurants****: Enjoy a meal at The Arrogant Butcher, located in downtown Phoenix, where local ingredients meet bold flavors. Another great spot for dining is Pizzeria Bianco, renowned for its artisanal pizzas.*
- ***Best Time of Year to Visit****: The cooler months from November to April are ideal for visiting Phoenix and enjoying indoor attractions like the museum without the intense summer heat.*
- ***Duration of Visit****: Plan to spend at least two to three hours at the museum to thoroughly enjoy its exhibitions and interactive displays.*
- ***Must-Do Experiences****: Ensure you visit the Governor's Office exhibit, restored to its 1909 appearance, offering a glimpse into the working environment of early Arizona governors. Also, check for special exhibitions or events, which are often held to commemorate significant anniversaries or historical events in Arizona's history.*

2.7: Lowell Observatory

Exploring the Cosmos

Lowell Observatory, located on Mars Hill in picturesque Flagstaff, Arizona, is more than simply a place of scientific discovery; it is a portal to the universe. Here, at one of the nation's oldest observatories, scientists found Pluto in 1930 and mapped the moon for the Apollo missions. It's a one-of-a-kind combination of historical sites, modern science, and stunning astronomical views where the secrets of the cosmos are unveiled right before your eyes.

A Legacy of Discovery

When people think of invention and exploration, they think of Lowell Observatory. It has been a pioneer in astronomy study since its founding in 1894 by Percival Lowell. Anyone interested in the cosmos will find this facility intriguing due to its historical importance and ongoing contributions to space science. Marry the same roads as the astronomers who have shifted our perspective on the cosmos and beyond.

Star-Gazing and Beyond

At the observatory, guests can take part in regular viewing sessions led by experienced astronomers who bring the glories of the night sky within reach of everybody. Solar telescopes provide a risk-free method of watching the sun during the day. There is always more to see and learn, whether you're using the Clark Telescope or exploring the interactive exhibits.

Engaging Programs and Events

There are many different kinds of educational activities and events held at Lowell Observatory all year round. Special viewing nights timed to coincide with major astronomical phenomena are among these, as are talks and seminars. Every one of these programs has one overarching goal: to inspire a love of science and astronomy among its participants.

Essential Details:

- ***Opening Hours and Admission Costs****: Lowell Observatory is open to the public from 10:00 AM to 10:00 PM, Monday through Saturday, and 10:00 AM to 5:00 PM on Sundays. Admission is $22 for adults, with discounts available for seniors, students, and children.*

- **Recommended Hotels**: *Consider staying at the Weatherford Hotel in downtown Flagstaff, offering historic charm with rates starting around $130 per night. It provides easy access to both the observatory and the city's vibrant downtown area.*
- **Recommended Restaurants**: *Treat yourself to a meal at Brix, which serves contemporary American cuisine with a focus on local, seasonal ingredients. For a more casual dining experience, try Diablo Burger for unique, locally sourced burgers.*
- **Best Time of Year to Visit**: *Flagstaff's clear skies make almost any time of year ideal for a visit, but summer and winter offer dramatic viewing opportunities for different celestial events.*
- **Duration of Visit**: *Plan to spend at least half a day at the observatory to enjoy both daytime and evening programs fully.*
- **Must-Do Experiences**: *Don't miss the chance to view celestial objects through the historic Clark Telescope, and be sure to participate in a guided night viewing session, where you can see distant galaxies, nebulae, and star clusters through powerful telescopes.*

Chapter 3: Native American Heritage in Arizona

3.1: Hopi Reservation – A Cultural Beacon

A Living Heritage

The Hopi Reservation, in northern Arizona's high desert plateaus, is a site where the past is both remembered and experienced in a very real way. This reservation provides an exceptional opportunity for tourists to learn about the Hopi culture, which is one of the oldest continuously existing civilizations in North America.

Cultural Insights

Experiencing life on the Hopi Reservation is like stepping into another world, where art, community, and spirituality are highly valued. Among the many Hopi arts and crafts, the most well-known are the elaborate kachina dolls, which are more than just decorative items; they are physical embodiments of the history and traditions of the Hopi people. Cultural centers and tours on the reservation, like the Hopi Cultural Center, shed light on the tribe's social structures, ceremonies, and deep connection to their ancestral land, in addition to these artistic traditions.

Spiritual Connections

Spiritual importance penetrates the environment of Hopi territory, which is revered as sacred. Ancient settlements like Walpi, where people still follow their traditional ways of life, can be explored on guided tours.

Offering an insight into Hopi cosmology and community rituals, these trips respectfully provide a look into the profound spiritual history that distinguishes the Hopi way of life.

Nature and Nurture

The natural environment of the Hopi Reservation is as stirring as its cultural components. The stark beauty of the desert, with its sweeping vistas and dramatic skies, complements the cultural journey visitors undertake. This land is not just a backdrop but a vital part of Hopi culture, fully integrated into their farming practices, art, and spiritual life.

Essential Details:

- ***Opening Hours and Admission Costs****: Access to the Hopi Reservation is regulated; all non-Hopi visitors must be accompanied by an official Hopi guide. Tour prices vary, generally starting around $70 per person for a half-day tour.*
- ***Recommended Hotels and Camping****: Stay at the Moenkopi Legacy Inn & Suites on the western edge of the reservation, with rooms averaging $130 per night. Camping options are limited on the reservation itself, but nearby Homolovi State Park offers facilities for $15-$30 per night.*
- ***Recommended Restaurants****: The Hopi Cultural Center Restaurant offers dishes made from traditional ingredients like blue corn and local meats. It's an excellent introduction to Hopi cuisine.*
- ***Best Time of Year to Visit****: Spring (April and May) and fall (September and October) are the best times to visit, offering mild weather and the opportunity to witness seasonal cultural events.*
- ***Duration of Visit****: Plan at least two days to explore the reservation, participate in a guided tour, and visit the cultural centers.*
- ***Must-Do Experiences****: Participate in a guided tour of the ancient village of Walpi, attend a cultural demonstration at the Hopi Cultural Center, and explore the mesas that define the landscape of the reservation.*

3.2: Tohono O'odham Nation – Guardians of the Sonoran Desert

Stewards of the Land

For generations, the Tohono O'odham people have made a home in the expansive Sonoran Desert, where they have been intrinsically linked to the earth and all its bounty. The Tohono O'odham people have developed a deep appreciation for their environment through their cultural practices, traditions, and sustainable resource management since they are custodians of this challenging yet dynamic ecosystem.

Cultural Richness

Basket weaving, ceramics, and other traditional arts and crafts of the Tohono O'odham Nation are world-renown for their aesthetic value and deep symbolic significance. Authentic Tohono O'odham music, dance, and art are showcased during the Nation's cultural events, which take place all year round and give visitors a glimpse into the heart of this long-lived culture.

Living Traditions

Native desert foods like cholla buds, saguaro fruit, and mesquite beans are an integral element of the Tohono O'odham diet, which is one of the most interesting parts of their culture. The Saguaro Fruit Harvest is one such annual event that showcases traditional cuisine and serves as a ritual to bring the community together, pass the knowledge down through the generations, and enjoy these meals.

Natural Connection

In the Tohono O'odham homelands, you can find native plants and animals in a wide variety of habitats, from steep mountains to expansive dry plains. They are spiritually and culturally bound to the soil, and this bond informs their environmental protection and farming methods.

Essential Details:

- ***Opening Hours and Admission Costs****: Visiting areas within the Tohono O'odham Nation often requires permission or a guide, as much of the land is protected and sacred. Specific events or cultural centers may have designated visiting hours and fees.*
- ***Recommended Hotels and Camping****: Stay at the Desert Diamond Casino Hotel in Tucson, offering comfortable*

accommodations with rates starting around $100 per night. For a closer experience to nature, consider camping in the nearby Organ Pipe Cactus National Monument, where sites are available at around $20 per night.

- **Recommended Restaurants**: *Try the Desert Rain Café in Sells, which specializes in dishes made from traditional Tohono O'odham ingredients, providing a taste of local cuisine.*
- **Best Time of Year to Visit**: *The best time to visit is during the cooler months from November to March, when the desert is more temperate and comfortable for exploration.*
- **Duration of Visit**: *Spend at least two days to appreciate the natural beauty of the lands and participate in any cultural events or tours.*
- **Must-Do Experiences**: *Participate in a guided tour to learn about the rich biodiversity of the Sonoran Desert, attend the Saguaro Fruit Harvest if visiting in late June, and explore the cultural exhibits at the Tohono O'odham Cultural Center and Museum to deepen your understanding of this unique nation.*

3.3: Yavapai-Prescott Indian Tribe – Heritage and Harmony

A Legacy of Resilience

Situated amidst verdant hills and picturesque scenery close to Prescott, Arizona, the Yavapai-Prescott Indian Tribe takes great pride in its rich legacy and the strength it has shown throughout its history. Although they are part of a modern community, the Yavapai people's rich traditions and practices are still respected and practiced.

Cultural Celebrations

Locals and tourists alike are welcomed to immerse themselves in the Yavapai-Prescott Tribe's vibrant cultural events, which showcase their rich traditions. The spiritual beliefs and historical journey of the tribe are brought to life via storytelling, traditional dance, and music at these gatherings. The yearly Pow Wow is a highlight because it showcases the Yavapai people's dynamic artistry and communal spirit through ceremonial dances and traditional dress.

Artistic Expressions

The tribe places a high value on art, and there are many talented local craftspeople who make baskets, jewelry, and pottery. Beautiful as they are, the Yavapai arts and crafts are rich in cultural meaning; each item represents a different facet of Yavapai life and philosophy. Visitors can see these artistic traditions up close and personal through the seminars and exhibitions hosted by the tribe's cultural center.

Harmony with Nature

The Yavapai homeland is a place that has always played an important role in the development of the Yavapai people. The area's abundance of natural resources is fundamental to the tribe's way of life, which includes making art and medicine from the materials they find there. The Yavapai people's dedication to protecting their land and water is on full display during guided nature walks that the tribe hosts, which shed light on these practices.

Essential Details:

- ***Opening Hours and Admission Costs***: *The tribe's cultural events and facilities typically welcome visitors during specific times of the year, especially during festivals. While there is no cost to enter the tribal lands, some events and facilities may charge a fee.*
- ***Recommended Hotels and Camping***: *Stay at the Prescott Resort and Conference Center, owned by the tribe, with rooms starting at around $150 per night. For those who prefer a closer connection to nature, the Point of Rocks RV Campground offers excellent facilities amidst stunning scenery, with rates starting from $45 per night.*
- ***Recommended Restaurants***: *The Prescott Resort offers a fine dining experience at its restaurant, which serves dishes inspired by native ingredients and traditional recipes. In downtown Prescott, The Raven Café provides a cozy ambiance and a menu of locally sourced, organic fare.*
- ***Best Time of Year to Visit***: *Spring (March to May) and fall (September to November) are ideal for visiting, offering mild weather perfect for outdoor activities and attending cultural events.*

- **Duration of Visit**: *Plan to spend at least two to three days in the area to fully engage with the community, participate in cultural experiences, and explore the natural beauty.*
- **Must-Do Experiences**: *Attend the annual Pow Wow if possible, participate in a guided tour of the tribe's cultural center, and join a nature walk to learn about the tribe's use of local plants for food and medicine.*

3.4: Pima-Maricopa Indian Community – Bridging Traditions and Modernity

A Fusion of Past and Present

A wonderful example of how traditional traditions and technological advancements may coexist, the Pima-Maricopa Indian Community is situated in the Sonoran Desert. Visitors to this village of Pima (Akimel O'odham) and Maricopa (Pee Posh) people will have the rare chance to immerse themselves in a centuries-old cultural mosaic.

Cultural Heritage Preserved

The Pima-Maricopa Indian Community is devoted to maintaining its culture by means of rituals, language, and art. At the center of these endeavors is the Cultural Center, which hosts programs and exhibits honoring the arts, history, and folklore of the indigenous peoples. To save traditional skills like beadwork, basket weaving, and ceramics from dying out, they are passed down from generation to generation.

Modern Vibrancy

They have a strong commitment to preserving their culture, but they have also welcomed modernization and are now in the forefront of economic development among Native American communities around the country. Modern enterprise and cultural celebration are showcased at Talking Stick Resort and Casino and Salt River Fields at Talking Stick. These facilities offer state-of-the-art amenities while maintaining native traditions.

Nature and Sustainability

For the Pima-Maricopa people, caring for the environment is fundamental. A profound reverence for the natural environment, regarded as a provider of life and a sacred entity, is at the heart of the community's endeavors in water conservation and sustainable agriculture. Learn about the indigenous peoples' land and resource management practices through educational programs and visits.

- **Opening Hours and Admission Costs**: *Many of the community's facilities and cultural sites have specific hours and may require an admission fee, particularly for guided tours and special exhibitions at the Cultural Center.*
- **Recommended Hotels and Camping**: *The Talking Stick Resort offers luxury accommodations with rooms starting at approximately $150 per night. Nearby, the Eagle View RV Resort provides high-quality amenities for those seeking a camping experience, with rates around $45 per night.*
- **Recommended Restaurants**: *Experience traditional dishes with a modern twist at the Orange Sky Restaurant atop the Talking Stick Resort, or enjoy casual dining with local ingredients at the Blue Coyote Café.*
- **Best Time of Year to Visit**: *The cooler months from October to April are ideal for visiting, when the desert heat subsides and the community's cultural events are most active.*
- **Duration of Visit**: *Spend at least two to three days in the community to fully experience the cultural offerings, engage with modern attractions, and explore the environmental initiatives.*
- **Must-Do Experiences**: *Take a guided tour of the Cultural Center to learn about the tribes' histories and crafts, try your hand at traditional basket weaving, and don't miss the chance to attend a cultural festival or community celebration if your visit coincides with these events.*

3.5: Havasupai Tribe – Guardians of the Grand Canyon

Stewards of a Hidden Oasis

The isolated home of the Havasupai people is nestled deep into the Grand Canyon's cracks. The grand canyon's beautiful waterfalls and clear waterways have been protected by the Havasupai, who are known as the "People of the Blue-Green Waters," for generations. One of the world's natural beauties is intertwined with the traditional culture of this community, and visiting their reserve gives a rare view into both.

Cultural Resilience

The Havasupai people have a strong bond to the region that their ancestors settled, which includes the breathtaking verdant waterfalls that bear their name. Interactions with tribal people and cultural exhibits allow visitors to delve into their rich oral traditions, ceremonies, and the craft of basket weaving. A strong tribute to the surviving spirit of the tribe is their history of perseverance, which includes battling land disputes and maintaining their traditions.

Nature's Marvels

Many tourists come to see the tribe's breathtaking natural scenery. Havasu Falls and Mooney Falls, two of the most famous waterfalls on the reservation, provide breathtaking scenery for outdoor enthusiasts and photographers. In this holy section of the Grand Canyon, you may expect an adventure typified by difficult paths and satisfying views.

Sustainable Tourism

The delicate balance between preserving the natural ecosystem and letting visitors enjoy Havasupai's beauty is achieved by well-managed tourism. To preserve their land for future generations, the tribe places an emphasis on sustainable tourism techniques.

Essential Details:

- ***Opening Hours and Admission Costs***: *Access to the Havasupai reservation is limited and requires reservations well in advance. Entrance fees, including camping and environmental fees, can total over $300 per person, depending on the length of stay.*
- ***Recommended Hotels and Camping***: *Lodging options within the reservation are limited to the Havasupai Lodge and designated camping areas near the waterfalls. Lodge rates start around $145 per night, while camping fees are included in the reservation package.*
- ***Recommended Restaurants***: *Dining options are limited within the reservation; visitors are advised to bring their own food supplies. The lodge and local vendors may offer some meals and basic provisions.*
- ***Best Time of Year to Visit***: *The best times to visit are from late spring to early fall when the weather is milder and the waterfalls are most vibrant.*

- **Duration of Visit**: *A typical visit lasts about 3 to 4 days, allowing ample time to hike to the falls, explore the area, and immerse in the natural beauty.*
- **Must-Do Experiences**: *Hike to Havasu Falls and Mooney Falls to witness their stunning turquoise waters, take part in a guided tour to learn about the tribe's history and culture, and spend a night under the stars at the campground to fully experience the tranquility of this isolated paradise.*

3.6: White Mountain Apache Tribe – Cultural Resilience in the High Country

A Legacy Amidst the Pines

The White Mountain Apache Tribe is a culturally rich and geographically large indigenous people that live in the expansive and verdant White Mountains of Arizona. In the midst of some of the most breathtaking Southwest landscapes, this tribe's history unfolds as a moving tale of perseverance, cultural preservation, and adaptation.

Cultural Heritage Preserved

The White Mountain Apache are cultural keepers whose lively ceremonies, arts, and customs are a window into the past. Artifacts, photographs, and artwork that depict the history of the Apache people from the past to the present provide visitors with insights into this heritage at the cultural center and museum of the tribe. An amazing cultural experience that exemplifies the spiritual profundity and communal ties of the Apache people is the Sunrise Dance, a rite of passage for young ladies.

Embracing Nature

The White Mountain Apache rely heavily on the natural environment. Expansive swaths of undeveloped territory are under the care of the tribe and provide a home for a wide variety of animals. Guided outdoor excursions, such as fishing in unspoiled rivers or hiking in hidden woodland paths, are examples of their sustainable methods and stewardship of the land.

Modern Contributions

The White Mountain Apache are known for their rich traditions, yet they are also very much a part of the modern world, actively contributing to the development of their territory. A resort and casino are only two of the many businesses run by the tribe; guests can relax in contemporary comforts while learning about the culture and helping the tribe make ends meet.

Essential Details:

- ***Opening Hours and Admission Costs****: The cultural center and museum are open to visitors year-round, with a small admission fee typically around $10 per person.*
- ***Recommended Hotels and Camping****: Stay at the Hon-Dah Resort Casino, which offers comfortable lodging starting at about $100 per night. For those seeking a closer connection with nature, nearby campgrounds in the Apache-Sitgreaves National Forests offer sites from $15 per night.*
- ***Recommended Restaurants****: The restaurant at Hon-Dah Resort provides a variety of dishes that include local specialties. Nearby Pinetop-Lakeside features several dining options like Charlie Clark's Steakhouse, known for its rustic setting and hearty meals.*
- ***Best Time of Year to Visit****: Summer and early fall are the best times to visit, offering mild weather and the chance to participate in outdoor activities and cultural events.*
- ***Duration of Visit****: Plan to spend at least three days to fully experience the natural beauty, cultural heritage, and modern amenities provided by the White Mountain Apache.*
- ***Must-Do Experiences****: Attend a Sunrise Dance ceremony if your visit coincides with this event, explore the natural beauty of the Fort Apache Historic Park, and take a guided wildlife watching tour to see native species in their natural habitats.*

Chapter 4: Outdoor Adventures in Arizona

4.1: Hiking and Backpacking in Arizona

The Grand Canyon: Bright Angel and South Kaibab Trails

Bright Angel and South Kaibab are two of the most famous hiking routes in the Grand Canyon, which is a natural wonder and one of the seven wonders of the world. Thanks to its mild descent and well-deserved reputation for historical importance, the Bright Angel Trail is perfect for hikers of all skill levels. There are covered rest houses and rest areas where you may get water. The South Kaibab Trail, on the other hand, is more hard but ultimately rewarding due to its higher terrain, panoramic views, and lack of water sources.

Havasupai Trail

Following the Havasupai Trail, which winds its way down into the Grand Canyon, visitors may see the breathtaking blue-green waterfalls on the Havasupai Indian Reservation. By providing insight into the daily lives of the Havasupai people, this trail serves as both a physical and cultural pilgrimage. The length and desert heat make the journey difficult, but the payoff of swimming in the perfect waters of Havasu Falls is unmatched.

Appalachian Trail

The Appalachian Trail is usually included when people talk about famous trails in the United States, even though it isn't in Arizona. Along its more than 2,000 miles, this trail passes through a wide range of landscapes and ecosystems in the eastern United States. Including it here sets a standard for the many hiking opportunities around the nation, including Arizona's vast trail networks.

Saguaro National Park

In southern Arizona, you'll find Saguaro National Park, which is perfect for desert adventurers because to its network of trails that wind through expansive cactus fields. The enormous saguaro cactus, indigenous to the Sonoran Desert, is the inspiration for the park's name.

Superstition Mountains

East of Phoenix, in the Superstition Mountains, you'll find trails that are full of history and tales. One of these is the one about the Lost Dutchman's Gold Mine. Hikers can enjoy the breathtaking scenery and a hint of intrigue on any of the several paths in these mountains, which vary in difficulty from moderate to very severe.

4.2: Rafting and Kayaking in Arizona

Grand Canyon Rafting

As it winds its way through the Grand Canyon, the Colorado River offers one of the world's most famous rafting adventures. From leisurely floats to exhilarating white-water rapids, this epic voyage might span a few days to three weeks. A once-in-a-lifetime adventure that mixes physical effort with scenic beauty awaits you in the river's mighty currents and stunning canyon views.

Lees Ferry to Diamond Creek

The rapids in this section of the river are world-famous, and they range from Class III to Class V. However, there are also serene sections where rafters may take in the majestic canyon walls and maybe even see some animals. It is common for knowledgeable guides to oversee these excursions, explaining the history of the region and making sure everyone stays safe.

Lake Powell Kayaking

Lake Powell, which straddles the Utah–Arizona border, is home to more than 2,000 miles of shoreline and innumerable canyons perfect for kayaking adventures. Paddlers seeking peace and quiet or a chance to fish in less traveled areas will find this area perfect due to its pristine waters and hidden coves.

Salt River Kayaking

The Salt River offers kayakers a chance to experience both calm waterways and difficult rapids, depending on the time of year and the water flow, for those who want a more exciting kayaking adventure. Many people go to the river to see wild horses and bald eagles, among other animals.

Environmental Conservation

Everyone who uses Arizona's waterways has a hand in keeping them in their immaculate condition. Paddlers are asked to adhere to the principles of Leave No Trace by disposing of all rubbish in a proper manner, applying sunscreen that is safe for the environment, and staying away from places that are environmentally fragile.

Educational Opportunities

In addition to rafting and kayaking trips, several outfitters provide educational programs that include topics including hydrology, ecology, and geology. By educating participants on the historical, ecological, and cultural importance of the places they are visiting, these programs enrich the experience.

4.3: Hot Air Ballooning in Arizona

Scenic Flights Over the Sonoran Desert

Hot air balloon rides over the Sonoran Desert, with its colorful sunsets and famous saguaro cacti, are a popular pastime. In the early morning, when the air is still and cooler and the sunrise casts a golden light over the desert, most balloon companies offer rides. Evening flights are less frequent, but they're just as beautiful, taking in the scenery as the sun sets gently over the horizon.

Sedona's Red Rocks

Ballooning is also a popular activity in Sedona, a town famous for its red sandstone formations. While gliding above Sedona, you can take in the city's iconic red rocks from above, as well as the canyons and fauna that inhabit them. As the sun moves across the sky, the pebbles change hues, creating a dynamic and fascinating visual experience.

Arizona Balloon Classic

Every year in the Phoenix region, hot air balloon aficionados congregate for the Arizona Balloon Classic. It's a weekend filled with racing, glows in the dark, and activities that the whole family can enjoy. Attendees will have the chance to see the sky illuminated with a kaleidoscope of colors when a large number of balloons take flight all at once.

Page-Lake Powell Balloon Regatta

The yearly balloon regatta in the Page-Lake Powell area provides a beautiful backdrop for those who enjoy ballooning to take in the breathtaking scenery of Glen Canyon and Lake Powell. A photographer's paradise is a scene where vibrant balloons reflect on the ocean.

Romantic and Group Adventures

Due to its personal and breathtaking location, hot air ballooning is frequently requested for romantic activities like marriage proposals or anniversary celebrations. For these kind of celebrations, a number of businesses provide private balloon rides, which can be upgraded with champagne toasts or gourmet brunches.

The fact that businesses can fit more people in their larger balloons makes group outings a popular choice. Whether it's a business event, a group of friends looking for an adventure, or a family reunion, these trips are sure to be a hit.

4.4: Off-Roading in Arizona

Apache Trail

State Route 88, more often known as the Apache Trail, is a well-known off-roading route in Arizona. Stunning vistas of the desert, canyons, and Roosevelt Lake are on display as it winds its way through the Superstition Mountains. The trail's steep dips, small roads, and combination of paved and unpaved sections make it difficult for even experienced drivers. Enjoy the stunning landscapes and rich history of Arizona, including ghost towns, Native American ruins, and abandoned mining camps, while off-roading in this area.

Sedona

In addition to its famous red rock scenery, Sedona is well-known for its extensive network of off-roading tracks suitable for drivers of varying abilities. For off-road enthusiasts, nothing beats the thrill of trails like Schnebly Hill Road, Broken Arrow, and Soldier Pass, which combine breathtaking scenery with exciting technical obstacles. Set against a breathtaking background of distinctive red rock formations and verdant foliage, this trip will be one you'll never forget.

Vehicle Types and Gear

All terrain vehicles (ATVs), utility vehicles (UTVs), and high-clearance 4x4s are all welcome on Arizona's off-road trails. You may find a number of local outfitters that provide guided trips and equipment rentals, making sure you have everything you need for a safe and pleasant experience. Because of their extensive experience and knowledge of the area, guided trips are ideal for individuals who are just starting out off-roading.

Events and Community

There is a thriving and inviting off-roading community in Arizona. The year is filled with events planned by many clubs and groups, such as skill clinics, clean-up days, and jamborees. Those new to off-roading can pick the brains of seasoned pros at these events, while those more experienced can share their love with others and learn more about the sport.

4.5: Rock Climbing in Arizona

Cochise Stronghold

Cochise Stronghold, in the Dragoon Mountains, is a sacred site because to the extreme cliffs and granite domes that surround it. Not only can you find great classic climbing routes in this Apache-historic region, but you can also explore deep canyons and untamed wildlife. Climbs here vary from short, sport routes to lengthy, traditional routes, and they all offer difficult yet rewarding trials.

Queen Creek Canyon

Queen Creek Canyon, next to Superior, is a popular climbing destination for people from the Phoenix region. Climbers of all skill levels and experience levels can choose from hundreds of routes on the site, which include both sport and classic routes. The excellent grips provided by the volcanic tuff and welded tuff make this a favorite among climbers of all skill levels.

Jack's Canyon

With more than 300 sport routes, Jack's Canyon on the Mogollon Rim region is a climber's paradise. Climbers of all skill levels will find something to their liking in this limestone sinkhole, which boasts routes up to 100 feet long with a difficulty range of 5.6 to 5.14. Climbers can fully immerse themselves in the tranquil, forested setting at the canyon, which is also a popular place to camp.

Climbing Seasons and Conditions

Climbing seasons in Arizona are mostly controlled by the weather. During the summer, places like Flagstaff in the north have cooler weather, while places like Tucson in the south have better weather in the fall, winter, and spring. Particularly in arid regions, where flash flooding is a real risk, climbers should constantly check the weather forecast before setting out, as abrupt changes might impact climbing safety.

Community and Resources

There is a thriving climbing culture in Arizona that is friendly to both novices and seasoned climbers. Indoor climbing facilities in Arizona communities like Flagstaff, Phoenix, and Tucson attract locals and visitors alike who come to socialize, exchange climbing advice, and plan group adventures. To help new climbers safely hone their abilities, many gyms and local businesses provide climbing lessons and guided excursions.

4.6: Wildlife Viewing in Arizona

Madera Canyon

Madera Canyon, in the Santa Rita Mountains to the south of Tucson, is well-known as a prime spot for birdwatching. As a stopover for migrating birds, it is also one of the best spots in the United States to spot uncommon species like elegant trogons. In addition to deer, black bears, and more than 250 bird species, the canyon is home to an astounding variety of other wildlife.

San Pedro Riparian National Conservation Area

One of the few surviving unspoiled desert riparian habitats in the United States is protected by this region, which is located near Sierra Vista. A vast array of species calls this area home, and it serves as an important resting place for migrating birds. It is a veritable birdwatcher's paradise, with over 400 species visible at any given time.

Ramsey Canyon Preserve

Located in the Huachuca Mountains and boasting the title of "Hummingbird Capital of the United States," Ramsey Canyon Preserve provides visitors with enough possibilities to see wildlife in a lush and verdant environment. The park is a haven for a variety of animals, including white-tailed deer, hummingbirds, and reptiles, but it really comes alive during the hummingbird migration season.

Saguaro National Park

Not only is the Sonoran Desert home to the world-famous saguaro cactus, but it is also an essential component of the ecosystem that provides food and shelter for many different kinds of animals. Gila monsters, coyotes, and a wide variety of birds, such as pygmy owls and cactus wrens, call this park home. The park's pathways are perfect for wildlife viewing, especially in the morning and late afternoon when the weather is milder and the animals are more active.

Organ Pipe Cactus National Monument

One of the best places to see the rare and exotic animals that call the Sonoran Desert home is this monument. The lesser long-nosed bat is an essential pollinator of the organ pipe cactus, and nighttime activities provide an opportunity to observe these species. During the day, guests have a chance to see a variety of lizards and desert bighorn sheep.

Engaging with Local Wildlife Experts

Wildlife excursions led by knowledgeable guides are available at many of Arizona's parks and preserves. In addition to improving the viewing experience, these trips can give light on the habits and environments of native species. Helping out with conservation efforts and learning more about Arizona's wildlife are two great benefits of taking part in these guided activities.

4.7: Skydiving in Arizona

Skydive Arizona in Eloy

Eloy is the site of Skydive Arizona, a world-renowned skydiving facility. The Arizona desert is a spectacular backdrop for Eloy's famous year-round jumps, which take place from heights of up to 13,000 feet. Tandem jumps, fast freefall programs, and a variety of training courses are available at this facility, making it suitable for skydivers of all skill levels.

Skydiving Over the Grand Canyon

Jumping out of a plane over the Grand Canyon is one of the most exciting and memorable experiences someone can have. Exciting adventurers can leap from specialized skydiving organizations in this area and witness one of the most renowned natural wonders from above. Enjoy the exhilaration of freefall while taking in breathtaking views of the canyon's natural beauty.

Tandem and Solo Jumps

Jumping from a height while tethered to a more experienced skydiving instructor is known as a tandem jump, and it's the most popular choice among beginners. With tandem skydiving, an experienced instructor takes care of the technical aspects of the jump while the participant relaxes and enjoys themselves, making it a popular choice among skydivers. Most skydiving centers provide extensive training programs that result in USPA (United States Parachute Association) certifications for individuals who wish to fly solo.

Special Events and Group Jumps

Birthdays, anniversaries, and corporate team-building events are just a few of the special occasions when skydiving is a popular choice. There are usually group discounts available for skydiving, and the groups can be as big or small as you like. Annual events are hosted by several skydiving centers and draw skydivers from all over the globe. These events include skill training, contests, and social gatherings.

The Thrill of the Experience

Skydiving is the most exhilarating sport there is. The sensation of freefall, the calmness of the parachute opening, and the slow descent are frequently characterized by jumpers as life-altering. Skydiving in Arizona is an exhilarating experience with some of the most breathtaking scenery in the nation, perfect for beginners and experienced alike.

4.8: Golfing in Arizona

Scottsdale and Phoenix

The two largest cities in Arizona, Scottsdale and Phoenix, are home to more than 200 golf courses. Whether you're a complete novice or a seasoned veteran, you'll find a course in one of these cities that suits your skill level. The Waste Management Phoenix Open, a highly anticipated event on the PGA Tour, is held each year at TPC Scottsdale, another notable course along with Troon North.

Tucson

The golf courses in Tucson are famous for both their scenic desert locations and the difficulty of the courses themselves. You may enjoy a round of golf and a stroll through some of the most beautiful parts of Arizona on courses like Ventana Canyon and Dove Mountain, which wind their way through breathtaking desert vistas.

Golfing Seasons and Conditions

The golfing season in Arizona is at its height in the winter and spring, when the weather is mild and pleasant. But Arizona's typically warm environment means that golf may be played at any time of year, unlike in many other states. Golfers love to get a head start on the day by playing a round first thing in the morning, before the temperature rises.

Golf Resorts and Accommodations

There are a number of Arizona golf courses that are attached to larger resorts that provide opulent lodgings and services. Perfect for golf trips, these resorts typically have spa treatments, gourmet restaurants, and other fun things to do. In addition to other high-end services, resorts like Scottsdale's Boulders Resort & Spa and Tucson's Loews Ventana Canyon Resort provide excellent golf.

Golfing Events and Tournaments

Golf enthusiasts in Arizona have the chance to witness the sport at its most elite level or even compete in tournaments themselves thanks to the abundance of amateur and professional events hosted by the state's courses throughout the year. The social impact of the sport is enhanced by these events, which often fund local charities and help to community development.

4.9: Tips for Your Arizona Adventures

Embarking on outdoor adventures in Arizona offers an unforgettable experience, thanks to the state's stunning landscapes and diverse environments. Whether you're planning to explore the vast deserts, climb the rugged mountains, or visit the lush forests, here are some essential tips to enhance your journey:

- *Stay Hydrated: Arizona's climate can be extremely dry, especially in the desert areas. Always carry plenty of water with you—more than you think you'll need—to prevent dehydration.*

- *Sun Protection: The sun in Arizona can be intense. Wear a broad-brimmed hat, sunglasses, and sunscreen with high SPF to protect your skin and eyes from harmful UV rays.*

- *Dress Appropriately: Layer your clothing. Even if the days are scorching, nights can be surprisingly cool, especially at higher elevations. Include light layers and a jacket in your packing list.*

- *Wildlife Awareness: Arizona is home to a variety of wildlife, including snakes, scorpions, and large mammals like bears and mountain lions. Be aware of your surroundings, especially when hiking or camping, and keep your distance from animals.*

- *Know the Rules: Many areas in Arizona, especially those on Native American reservations or protected lands, have specific visiting rules and regulations. Research and respect these guidelines, including obtaining necessary permits for activities like hiking, camping, or fishing.*

- *Travel with Maps: While digital navigation tools are incredibly useful, having physical maps of the areas you're visiting is invaluable, especially in remote locations where cell service may be spotty.*

- *Leave No Trace: Preserve the natural beauty of Arizona by following Leave No Trace principles. Pack out all your trash, stay on designated trails, and avoid disturbing wildlife or natural habitats.*

- *Timing Your Visit: Plan your outdoor activities in the early morning or late afternoon to avoid the midday heat, especially during the summer months. Additionally, visiting popular spots on weekdays can help you avoid large crowds.*

- *Emergency Preparedness: Carry a basic first aid kit, know the signs of heat exhaustion and heat stroke, and inform someone of your travel plans, especially if venturing into less populated or rugged areas.*

- **Cultural Sensitivity**: *When visiting areas rich in Native American heritage, such as tribal lands or national monuments, show respect for local customs and traditions. This might mean observing restrictions on photography or participating in guided tours to gain a deeper understanding of the cultural significance of these places.*
- **Seasonal Considerations**: *Be mindful of the season during which you plan your trip. Spring and fall are generally the best times to explore outdoor Arizona, offering mild weather and vibrant natural displays.*

Chapter 5: Arizona's Urban Delights

5.1: Phoenix – A Blend of Culture, Nature, and Innovation

Phoenix Rising: A Dynamic Metropolis

Travelers from all over the globe flock to Phoenix, the sun-kissed capital of Arizona, to experience its dynamic mix of culture, nature, and innovative spirit. Phoenix is an inviting city that offers a diverse range of activities, from lively art districts to peaceful desert settings.

Cultural Heartbeat

Just like the city's geography, Phoenix's cultural scene is very diversified. The Phoenix Art Museum is a great place to immerse yourself in local art because of its remarkable collection, which spans the years 1500 to the present. The Herberger Theater Center is a great place to experience local theater. On the first Friday of every month, galleries in the Roosevelt Row Arts District open their doors to the public for a joyous art and community festival known as the First Fridays Art Walk.

Nature's Bounty

There is a plethora of breathtaking scenery in Phoenix. In particular, the spring blossoms in the Desert Botanical Garden provide a breathtaking display of form and color, showcasing the incredible diversity of desert vegetation. South Mountain Park's paths offer thrill seekers a difficult way to get away from it all while still taking in breathtaking vistas of the city.

Innovation Hub

Phoenix is at the forefront of environmental and technological advancement. Learn about science in a way that everyone can understand and enjoy by visiting the Arizona Science Center and exploring their interactive displays. Community projects like urban gardens and water conservation programs, as well as solar-powered public areas, demonstrate the city's dedication to sustainable living.

Essential Details:

- ***Recommended Hotels***: *The Kimpton Hotel Palomar in downtown Phoenix offers stylish accommodations with a rooftop pool and spectacular city views, starting around $150 per night. For a budget-friendly option, consider the Clarendon Hotel and Spa, known for its excellent service and vibrant decor, with rooms averaging $120 per night.*
- ***Recommended Restaurants***: *Phoenix's culinary scene is booming. Enjoy farm-to-table dishes at FnB, where the menu highlights Arizona's agricultural bounty. For a taste of authentic Mexican cuisine, don't miss Barrio Café, celebrated for its fresh guacamole and vibrant murals.*
- ***Best Time of Year to Visit***: *Visit from November to April, when the weather is cool and sunny, perfect for exploring both the city and the surrounding desert.*

- **Duration of Visit**: *Allocate at least three to four days to experience the best of Phoenix's cultural exhibits, natural beauty, and innovative projects.*
- **Must-Do Experiences**: *Hike to the summit of Camelback Mountain at sunrise for breathtaking views, explore the historic architecture of the Heard Museum, and relax in the serene Japanese Friendship Garden.*

5.2: Tucson – A Hub of History, Arts, and Natural Beauty

Where Cultures Converge

More than just a metropolis, Tucson, Arizona, is a living fabric of diverse cultures, creative expressions, and stunning natural scenery. As you meander through this sun-kissed metropolis, you'll get to know its spirit in the vast desert that envelops it, its soul in the Spanish missions, and its heartbeat in the thriving local markets.

Historic Landmarks and Cultural Treasures

The restored façade of the Barrio Viejo district and the historic mission of San Xavier del Bac, an impressive example of Spanish colonial architecture, are tangible manifestations of Tucson's vibrant history. Native American, Spanish, Mexican, and Anglo influences have molded the city's complex history, and each structure reveals a different story of convergence and transformation.

A Thriving Arts Scene

In Tucson, art is flourishing. Local artists display a wide range of work in the city's galleries, from realistic landscapes to abstract modernism. Attracting artists and collectors from all over the globe, the annual Tucson Gem and Mineral Show turns the city into a global platform for natural beauty. Venues in Tucson play host to indie bands as well as Broadway tours, demonstrating the city's dedication to the arts.

Nature's Canvas

The cultural scene in Tucson is captivating, but the natural world is much more so. With its towering cacti guarding the Sonoran Desert, Saguaro National Park encircles the city's outskirts. Trails for hikers wind across springtime vistas adorned with flaming wildflowers. The Arizona-Sonora Desert Museum, located just outside of town, is a living museum showcasing the varied plant and animal life that makes its home in this beautiful but unforgiving desert.

- **Recommended Hotels and Camping**: *The historic Hotel Congress offers rooms starting at $99, providing a taste of 1930s Tucson. For a closer-to-nature experience, Gilbert Ray Campground offers amenities with desert views for about $20 per night.*
- **Recommended Restaurants**: *Tucson is famous for its Mexican cuisine. Don't miss the Sonoran-style dishes at El Charro Café, or enjoy innovative desert-inspired meals at The Tasteful Kitchen.*
- **Best Time of Year to Visit**: *Fall through spring offers pleasant temperatures ideal for exploring both the city and the surrounding desert.*
- **Duration of Visit**: *Spend at least three days to soak in the historical sites, art, and natural beauty.*
- **Must-Do Experiences**: *Catch a sunrise or sunset at Saguaro National Park, explore the historic artifacts at the Arizona State Museum, and if you're visiting in February, don't miss the Tucson Gem and Mineral Show.*

5.3: Scottsdale – A Blend of Luxury, Culture, and Natural Beauty

A City of Sophistication

Renown as "The West's Most Western Town," Scottsdale, Arizona, provides an unparalleled fusion of opulent lifestyles, thriving cultural scenes, and breathtaking natural scenery. Indulge in the city's grandeur while discovering its inventive spirit and world-class resorts, art galleries, and breathtaking outdoor areas.

Cultural Richness

Visit the many art galleries in Scottsdale, particularly along Main Street, to immerse yourself in the city's vibrant cultural environment. Enjoy a wide range of live performances at the Scottsdale Center for the Performing Arts, including theater, music, and dance, featuring both local and worldwide talent. The Scottsdale Museum of Contemporary Art (SMoCA) offers thought-provoking displays of modern art.

Luxury Redefined

Resorts and spas in Scottsdale are among the best in the Southwest, and the city itself is a byword for opulence. Both the Fairmont Scottsdale Princess and the Phoenician offer more than simply a place to sleep; guests may indulge in a variety of high-end amenities, such as spa treatments, golf, and fine dining.

Natural Beauty

In addition to its many urban attractions, Scottsdale serves as a gateway to the stunning natural vistas of the Sonoran Desert. Hikers, bikers, and equestrians will love the more than 200 miles of trails in the McDowell Sonoran Preserve, which wind through breathtaking desert landscapes. You can find a peaceful morning stroll or an exciting adventure along the preserve's pathways, which lead you into the breathtaking desert landscape.

Essential Details:

- **Recommended Hotels**: *Stay at the luxurious Scottsdale Resort at McCormick Ranch with rooms starting at $200 per night, or enjoy the rustic charm of Four Seasons Resort Scottsdale with average rates of $300 per night.*
- **Recommended Restaurants**: *Dine at FnB, where the locally-sourced menu highlights Arizona's agricultural community, or experience the vibrant atmosphere and modern Mexican cuisine at La Hacienda by Richard Sandoval.*
- **Best Time of Year to Visit**: *Visit from November to April to enjoy cooler weather, ideal for exploring both the cultural attractions and natural landscapes.*
- **Duration of Visit**: *Plan to spend at least three days to experience the cultural highlights and natural beauty of Scottsdale fully.*
- **Must-Do Experiences**: *Explore the galleries during the Scottsdale ArtWalk, relax in the serene Desert Botanical Garden, and take a sunset horseback ride through the McDowell Sonoran Preserve.*

5.4: Sedona – A Sanctuary of Natural Splendor and Spiritual Renewal

A Haven of Beauty and Serenity

More than just a beautiful scenery, Sedona, Arizona's red rock formations and energetic vortexes provide a haven for individuals in search of serenity and rejuvenation. Artists, healers, and ecotourists from all over the globe go to this magical city for its unparalleled beauty and mysterious abilities.

Art and Soul

A vibrant arts scene encapsulates the essence of Sedona. A wide variety of art forms, from Native American wares to modern masterpieces, are on display in the downtown galleries. One example is the Sedona Gallery Association's 1st Friday in the Galleries, a monthly event that showcases the town's artistic talents and offers a fun space for visitors to meet local artists.

Spiritual Retreat

The spiritual offerings in Sedona attract many visitors. Many people believe that the area's energy vortexes can help with healing and meditation, and they offer a special place to come here to connect with one's spirituality and reflect on one's life. Immersive experiences that make use of the natural environment to inspire and revitalize are offered by guided spiritual tours and wellness retreats.

Outdoor Adventures

The red rock scenery of Sedona is a fantastic place for adventure seekers. Fantastic vistas and an opportunity to interact with the tranquil, powerful energy of the land are offered by trails for all abilities, such as the easy-going Bell Rock Pathway and the demanding Cathedral Rock Trail. A unique vantage point over this breathtaking area is offered by early morning hot air balloon tours.

Essential Details:

- ***Recommended Hotels and Camping***: *El Portal Sedona Hotel offers a luxury boutique experience with rooms starting around $250 per night. For a closer-to-nature stay, Rancho Sedona RV Park provides beautiful creekside camping spots with amenities starting at $45 per night.*

- **Recommended Restaurants**: *Enjoy a meal at Mariposa Latin Inspired Grill, where you can dine with panoramic views of Sedona's red rocks. For a casual yet memorable breakfast or lunch, the Coffee Pot Restaurant is famous for its 101 omelets and Southwestern hospitality.*
- **Best Time of Year to Visit**: *Spring (March to May) and fall (September to November) are the best times to visit Sedona, offering mild weather and the natural beauty of changing seasons.*
- **Duration of Visit**: *Spend at least three to four days to explore the art, nature, and spiritual offerings of Sedona thoroughly.*
- **Must-Do Experiences**: *Don't miss the opportunity to experience a sunrise or sunset yoga session on the rocks, explore the backcountry on a Jeep tour, and visit the Chapel of the Holy Cross, a stunning architectural landmark built into the buttes.*

5.5: Flagstaff – A Blend of Natural Wonders and Vibrant Culture

Gateway to the Grand Outdoors

Located in Arizona's Coconino National Forest, the charming town of Flagstaff is known for its stunning landscapes and exciting nightlife. Outdoor enthusiasts and culture vultures alike will find paradise in Flagstaff, Arizona, thanks to its temperate climate, pine-covered mountains, and closeness to some of the state's most breathtaking natural attractions.

Cultural Melting Pot

The cultural environment in Flagstaff is lively and diversified, just like the city itself. Among the many cultural events held annually in Flagstaff are the Flagstaff Music Festival and the Flagstaff Festival of Science, both of which honor the city's devotion to the arts and sciences. The downtown area is a haven for artists, both local and visiting, thanks to its abundance of galleries and live music venues.

Outdoor Adventures Abound

The city is a jumping off point for excursions to nearby natural attractions like Sedona's breathtaking red rocks and the Grand Canyon, which is about an hour away by car. The San Francisco Peaks, which are closer to town, include routes that are suitable for hikers of all abilities, while the Arizona

Snowbowl is a great place to go skiing in the winter and hiking in the summer with breathtaking views. Nearby Walnut Canyon National Monument provides an opportunity to see prehistoric cliff houses in a breathtaking canyon setting.

A Hub for Astronomy

Lowell Observatory, the site of Pluto's discovery, is located near Flagstaff, which contributes to the city's reputation for astronomy and its dark sky. Visitors can look at cosmic wonders through vintage and modern telescopes during the nightly viewing sessions hosted by the observatory.

Essential Details:

- *Recommended Hotels and Camping: The Little America Hotel offers a luxurious stay amidst 500 acres of beautiful forest, with rates starting at $150 per night. For those who prefer to sleep under the stars, the Pine Flat Campground near Sedona offers excellent facilities in a picturesque setting for about $25 per night.*
- *Recommended Restaurants: Brix Restaurant and Wine Bar serves contemporary American cuisine made from locally sourced ingredients. For a more casual experience, the Lumberyard Brewing Company offers hearty pub fare alongside a selection of craft beers brewed on-site.*
- *Best Time of Year to Visit: The best times to visit Flagstaff are from May to October when the weather is warm and all trails are open. Winter brings its own charm with snowy landscapes perfect for skiing and snowboarding.*
- *Duration of Visit: Plan to spend at least three days in Flagstaff to fully explore the natural beauty, cultural sites, and historical attractions.*
- *Must-Do Experiences: Don't miss a trip to the Grand Canyon, an evening of stargazing at Lowell Observatory, and a hike through the lava tubes at Sunset Crater Volcano National Monument.*

5.6: Tempe – A Vibrant Hub of Innovation and Recreation

Dynamic and Diverse

Tempe, Arizona, is a great place to live because of its lively vibe, innovative spirit, and plenty of things to do. It's in the Valley of the Sun. Tempe,

Arizona, is a vibrant metropolis that is home to Arizona State University and a crossroads of cultures, technologies, and entertainment.

Cultural and Educational Center

The cultural landscape of Tempe is just as vibrant as its people. Tempe Town Lake is home to the Tempe Center for the Arts, which showcases the artistic diversity of the city via a wide range of productions in theater, music, and dance. Students' dynamic productions and state-of-the-art research make the Arizona State University campus a hive of creativity that adds to the city's exciting atmosphere.

Outdoor Activities Galore

Tempe Town Lake is the ideal spot for outdoor recreation in Tempe, with its picturesque bike and jogging routes, kayaking and paddleboarding opportunities, and more. Papago Park, which is close by, has a rocky terrain that's great for trekking and has family-friendly activities like the Desert Botanical Garden and Phoenix Zoo.

Thriving Nightlife and Culinary Scene

Tempe is well-known for more than only its cuisine and nightlife. Every taste can be satisfied at one of the many restaurants, from quaint cafés to lively brewpubs and even fine dining establishments. Located in the middle of Tempe's vibrant nightlife, Mill Avenue is home to a wide variety of eateries, stores, and bars that keep the party going well into the wee hours.

Essential Details:

- ***Recommended Hotels****: Stay at the Tempe Mission Palms Hotel, conveniently located near downtown and ASU, with rates starting around $150 per night. For more budget-friendly options, the MOXY Phoenix Tempe offers a trendy atmosphere with rooms averaging $100 per night.*
- ***Recommended Restaurants****: Don't miss Culinary Dropout at The Yard for a unique dining experience with live music and classic games, or enjoy the waterfront views at The Watershed, known for its local cuisine and vibrant atmosphere.*
- ***Best Time of Year to Visit****: The best times to visit Tempe are from September to November and from February to April when the weather is mild and perfect for outdoor activities.*

- **Duration of Visit**: *A weekend in Tempe is typically sufficient to explore the major attractions, enjoy some outdoor activities, and dive into the local food scene.*
- **Must-Do Experiences**: *Take a paddleboard or kayak out on Tempe Town Lake, explore the hiking trails at Papago Park, and enjoy an evening of entertainment and dining on Mill Avenue.*

5.7: Mesa – A Cultural and Recreational Oasis in the Desert

Dynamic Urban Culture

In the middle of the desert lies Mesa, Arizona, a thriving cultural center. Immerse yourself in the vibrant environment of Mesa, a city that welcomes both visitors and locals with its rich history, arts, and numerous recreational opportunities. The broad assortment of experiences offered by Mesa's many museums, artistic venues, and distinctive cultural events is sure to please visitors of all ages and interests.

Cultural Celebrations and Artistic Flair

The Mesa Arts Center, the biggest arts and entertainment park in the Southwest, is just one of several galleries and performing venues that showcase the city's commitment to the arts. Visitors can enjoy live music, art exhibitions, and theater shows all year round at this venue. Festivals such as the Mesa Music Festival, which hosts both regional and national performers, further enhance the cultural landscape.

Recreational Haven

There are a plethora of recreational opportunities on Mesa, so it's not just about culture. Visitors may enjoy a variety of outdoor activities, including hiking, biking, and water sports, thanks to its close vicinity to the Tonto National Forest and the Salt River. Numerous parks and community centers provide a variety of events and activities, and there are plenty of greens for golfers to practice on.

A Community Focused on Education and Innovation

Several colleges and universities in Mesa contribute to the city's culture of learning and creativity, demonstrating the importance of education to the local population. The city's vibrant personality and robust economy are supported by these institutions.

Essential Details:

- **Recommended Hotels and Camping**: *Consider staying at the Mesa Grand Hotel, with rooms starting at $120 per night, or enjoy the outdoors at the Mesa Spirit RV Resort, where sites average $40 per night.*
- **Recommended Restaurants**: *Dine at the award-winning TQLA Mesa, known for its Southwestern cuisine, or enjoy the family-friendly atmosphere at Bobby Q's BBQ.*
- **Best Time of Year to Visit**: *The best times to visit Mesa are from March to May and from October to November, when the weather is mild and perfect for outdoor activities.*
- **Duration of Visit**: *A minimum of three days is recommended to fully experience the cultural and recreational activities Mesa has to offer.*
- **Must-Do Experiences**: *Don't miss exploring the Mesa Historical Museum, taking a scenic hike through Usery Mountain Regional Park, and catching a performance at the Mesa Arts Center.*

5.8: Chandler – A Modern Blend of Innovation, Culture, and Recreation

A Thriving Urban Oasis

Chandler, Arizona, exemplifies how a community can combine innovation, cultural diversity, and abundant recreational options to form a vibrant and prosperous metropolitan setting. Chandler, a city in the greater Phoenix area, is known for its sun-kissed landscapes and community-oriented lifestyle, as well as its distinctive blend of high-tech industry and lively cultural life.

Cultural Heartbeat

Chandler hosts a wide variety of events and places that honor many parts of human creativity, demonstrating its dedication to cultural diversity. One of the most important venues for this kind of artistic expression is the Chandler Center for the Arts, which hosts a diverse array of shows and performances by national and international artists. As a reflection of the city's diverse population, multicultural festivals such as the Chandler Multicultural Festival and the Chandler Indian Art Market feature a wide array of international art, music, and cuisine.

Innovative Spirit

Not content to merely hold on to its traditions, this city is actively working to create new ones via innovation. Chandler is house to some of the most innovative software, manufacturing, and sustainability-focused tech companies in the country. Free Wi-Fi zones and community centers with integrated technology attract families and young professionals alike, demonstrating the city's tech-savvy attitude in public places.

Recreational Paradise

A wide variety of recreational opportunities dot Chandler's terrain. Many parks, pools, and miles of bike lanes make this city a great place to get some exercise. Golfers will discover an abundance of courses to test their abilities, and families will find several opportunities to come together through various community activities and sports leagues.

Essential Details:

- ***Recommended Hotels and Camping****: Stay at the luxurious Crowne Plaza Phoenix-Chandler Golf Resort, where the average rate is about $160 per night, offering prime access to downtown and local golf courses. For those seeking a more natural retreat, the nearby Desert Breeze RV Park provides excellent facilities and quick city access for around $30 per night.*
- ***Recommended Restaurants****: Indulge in some of the best steaks in town at DC Steak House, or enjoy authentic Mexican flavors at El Zocalo Mexican Grille.*
- ***Best Time of Year to Visit****: Ideal times to visit Chandler are during the fall (September to November) and spring (March to May), when the weather is perfect for both indoor and outdoor activities.*
- ***Duration of Visit****: A weekend in Chandler is usually sufficient to explore the major attractions, but extending your stay to a week allows for a deeper exploration of the city's parks and cultural offerings.*
- ***Must-Do Experiences****: Don't miss the Chandler Jazz Festival if you're visiting in the spring, and make sure to explore the Veterans Oasis Park, which not only offers trails and wildlife viewing but also serves as an environmental education center.*

Chapter 6: Arizona's Unique Festivals and Events And Culinary Delights

6.1: The Tucson Gem and Mineral Show: A Desert Treasure

As the world's biggest, oldest, and most esteemed gem and mineral display, the Tucson Gem and Mineral display, takes place every winter, the dynamic city of Tucson becomes a worldwide community. In addition to being a marketplace, this event—fondly called the "Jewel of the Desert"—celebrates natural history, beauty, and the art of collecting. Treasures that intrigue collectors, scientists, and enthusiasts abound in the show, including dazzling geodes, rare jewels, and elaborate jewelry. Anyone with even a passing interest in the natural world should make it a point to stop by the Tucson Gem and Mineral Show. It's like stepping into a magical universe where the Earth's deepest mysteries are on exhibit.

Key Details of the Tucson Gem and Mineral Show

- ***Event Timing:*** *Annually, typically held over two weeks in late January to early February.*
- ***Admission Fees:*** *Varies by venue; main show typically under $20 for adults with discounts for children, seniors, and military personnel.*
- ***Duration:*** *Main event spans four days, but related shows occur over approximately two weeks.*

6.2: Arizona Renaissance Festival: Time Travel to the 16th Century

The Arizona Renaissance Festival will transport you to a bygone era through a cacophony of sights, sounds, and tastes. Standing tall in Apache Junction, this yearly extravaganza transports attendees to a European village teeming with gallant knights, joyful minstrels, and jesters. Indulge in jousting in the lists, witness a falcon take flight, and chow down on a gigantic turkey leg—all while enjoying this festival's blend of history and nonstop entertainment. It's a magical getaway for families, history lovers, and anybody else seeking a touch of enchantment in their contemporary lives.

Essential Details: for Festival Goers

- **Time of Year:** *The festival runs annually, typically starting in February and continuing through March.*
- **Admission Costs:** *Ticket prices are generally around $28 for adults and $18 for children, with discounts available for advance purchase.*
- **Event Duration:** *The festival is open on weekends during its run, from 10 AM to 6 PM, rain or shine.*

6.3: Scottsdale Arabian Horse Show: A Spectacle of Grace and Tradition

The city of Scottsdale is always bustling with activity during the Scottsdale Arabian Horse Show, an event that has expanded from a modest gathering in 1955 to become the biggest Arabian horse show in the world. Over 2,400 Arabian and half-Arabian horses compete for honors and great awards at this renowned event. In addition to getting a close look at the magnificent animals, spectators may enjoy a number of horse shows, including halter, jumping, and dressage. A cultural event featuring educational lectures, a shopping expo, and live entertainment, the show is more than simply horse competitions. It's a great place for families or anybody interested in horses to visit. Indulge in a day of passionate competition and equestrian elegance while marveling at the speed and grace of these magnificent creatures.

Essential Details: of the Scottsdale Arabian Horse Show

- **Event Timing:** *Annually in February, typically spanning over 11 days.*

- **Admission Fees:** *General admission is around $10 per day, with options for reserved seating and multi-day passes available at additional costs.*
- **Duration:** *The event lasts for 11 days, offering a full schedule of competitions, exhibitions, and special events.*

6.4: Sedona International Film Festival: A Canvas for Independent Spirit

Set against the backdrop of Sedona's famous red rock vistas, the Sedona International Film Festival is a refuge for lovers of indie cinema and a symbol of innovation. The picturesque town transforms into a hive of activity every year as filmmakers, cinema lovers, and storytellers from all over the world descend upon it for this festival. In addition to screenings, the festival offers a full immersion experience with workshops, panels, and talks with artists and creators, creating a supportive environment for independent filmmakers to showcase their work and for audiences to delve deeply into the artistic aspects of cinema. The festival's exciting vibe and beautiful setting provide an outstanding cultural experience for cinema buffs and non-moviegoers alike.

Event Details:
- **Event Timing:** *Held annually, usually in late February.*
- **Admission Fees:** *Ticket prices vary, with options ranging from single film tickets to full festival passes. Average single screening tickets are around $15, while full passes can exceed $200 for access to all events and premieres.*
- **Duration:** *The festival spans nine days, filled with film screenings, workshops, and celebrity panels.*

6.5: Experience the Heartbeat of Arizona at the State Fair

A flurry of tradition, community pride, and excitement is brought to Phoenix every fall by the Arizona State Fair. The grandeur of amusement rides, the scent of fried food, the sounds of laughing and live music combine to create a memorable ambiance at this exuberant event. With its rich history in Arizona, this fair highlights the state's finest through exciting livestock shows, contests, and nighttime music. The Grand Canyon State is home to a diverse array of towns and cultures, and the fairgrounds provide an opportunity for people of all ages to come together, delve into exciting adventures, and make new memories. It's a celebration of Arizona's culture and heritage, not merely a fair.

Event Details:

- **Event Timing:** *Held annually in the fall, typically starting in early October and running through the end of the month.*
- **Admission Fees:** *General admission is around $12 for adults, with discounts available for seniors, children, and various promotional days.*
- **Duration:** *The fair lasts for about three weeks, providing ample opportunity to explore all its facets at your leisure.*

6.6: Prescott Frontier Days – A Western Experience to Remember

Prescott Frontier Days is where you may experience the "World's Oldest Rodeo" and relive the exciting days of the Old West. This Fourth of July celebration has been taking place in the charming Arizona town of Prescott since 1888 and features a diverse array of events, including rodeo competitions, cultural celebrations, and community pride. Enjoy the heart-pounding rodeo events sanctioned by the Professional Rodeo Cowboys Association, where you can witness the best athletes from around the country compete in thrilling sports like bull riding and barrel racing. Each and every one of the event's attendees will get a taste of the American West thanks to the big parade, the Western art display, and the many educational events that are part of the celebration. For those seeking a genuine taste of American cowboy culture, this event is more than simply a rodeo; it is an integral part of the cultural and community calender of Prescott.

Event Details:

- **Time of Year:** *Annually around the Fourth of July*
- **Admission Prices:** *Ticket prices vary; attendees should check the event's official website for the most current pricing information.*
- **Event Duration:** *The festivities span several days, culminating in the rodeo events and parade.*

6.7: Tucson Festival of Books – A Literary Celebration

The Tucson Festival of Books is more than just a gathering; it is a lively ode to literature that inspires both authors and readers. Located at Tucson's University of Arizona, this event becomes a hive of activity as writers, publishers, and bookworms from across the nation assemble to celebrate literature's enchantment. Everyone is sure to find something of interest at this literary festival, which features engaging panel discussions as well as practical workshops.

Event Details:

- **Time of Year:** *The Tucson Festival of Books takes place annually, typically during the springtime when the desert blooms with life.*
- **Price:** *Admission to this literary wonderland won't break the bank—it's often affordable or even free, ensuring that literature remains accessible to all.*
- **Duration:** *Prepare for a weekend filled to the brim with literary delights as the festival spans across multiple days, giving attendees ample time to soak in the literary atmosphere.*

6.8: Flagstaff Folk Festival – A Celebration of Folk Music and Community

The Flagstaff Folk Festival, a lively celebration of folk music and community fellowship, is a magnet for those seeking a slice of northern Arizona. This yearly celebration pays beautiful tribute to the diverse array of folk customs through lively music and elaborate handicrafts.

Event Details:

- **Season:** *Held during the balmy days of summer, usually in late June or early July, when the sun casts a warm glow over Flagstaff's picturesque landscape.*
- **Price:** *Affordable for all, with ticket options catering to various budgets and preferences, ensuring that everyone can join in the festivities.*
- **Duration:** *Spanning over a weekend, the festival offers ample time for attendees to immerse themselves in the melodic melodies, insightful workshops, and vibrant marketplace.*

6.9: Arizona's Culinary Delights

Traditional Southwestern flavors, Mexican influences, and modern culinary innovations come together in Arizona's dynamic and diversified culinary scene, much like the state's landscapes. From traditional regional fare to more modern eateries that serve the refined tastes of our intended audience, this chapter delves into the diverse culinary landscape of Arizona.

Southwestern Cuisine

Bold flavors and native ingredients like chiles, corn, and beans define Southwestern cuisine, which is a trademark of Arizona's culinary identity. The Three Sisters Stew—a combination of corn, beans, and squash—and Frybread, a classic Native American flatbread, are just a few examples of the dishes that showcase the culinary ingenuity and agricultural heritage of the area.

Mexican Flavors

The closeness of Arizona to Mexico has a profound effect on its food, bringing with it tastes and ingredients that are now staples all around the state. Local and tourists alike can enjoy dishes like Bison Chili and Acorn Bread, which combine traditional Mexican culinary techniques with ingredients from the area.

Craft Beer and Microbreweries

Microbreweries in Arizona are responsible for the state's thriving craft beer scene, which features everything from classic lagers to unique ales. Here we take a look at some of the best breweries in the state and the beers they make, showcasing the ways in which new brewing techniques and regional tastes have shaped the state's thriving beer scene.

Wine Tasting in Arizona

Vineyards in Arizona's Verde Valley and Southern Arizona, among others, have become famous for their excellent wines. The wine tasting experience is explored in this part, along with vineyards and wines that showcase the region's distinctive terroir.

Farm-to-Table Experiences

Many Arizona restaurants and stores adhere to the farm-to-table philosophy by exclusively serving foods that are grown or raised inside the state. Fresh, savory meals showcasing the finest of the season are guaranteed thanks to this trend, which also helps Arizona's agricultural community.

Sonoran Hot Dogs and Chimichangas

Popular dishes in the area include deep-fried burritos called Chimichangas and bacon-wrapped Sonoran Hot Dogs that are stuffed with beans, onions, and sauces. These dishes showcase the vibrant and adventurous nature of Arizona's food culture, with flavors that are just as lively and daring as the state itself.

Chapter 7: Essential Travel Tips for Arizona

The Grand Canyon and the thriving art scenes of Phoenix and Tucson are just two of the many breathtaking natural attractions and culturally diverse experiences that Arizona has to offer. To assist tourists make the most of their time in this culturally rich state, this chapter includes must-read travel advice. Travelers can plan an efficient and enjoyable Arizona journey with practical tips on the best times to travel, lodging options, transportation, and safety.

Best Time to Visit

Think about the weather where you're going in Arizona so you can make the most of the outdoors. The weather is pleasant and perfect for outdoor activities like hiking, sightseeing, and attending festivals throughout the spring (March to May) and fall (September to November) seasons. The desert regions of Arizona may get very hot in the summer, so it's better to avoid outdoor activities during the middle of the day if you can.

Getting Around Arizona

Having a personal vehicle is highly advised when visiting Arizona's vast landscapes and distant sites. At most major airports in Arizona, you can rent a car for your trip into the state. Renting a recreational vehicle (RV) could be a convenient and affordable option for long-term travelers, especially those interested in seeing rural areas and national parks. Buses and light rail systems are available for public transit in major cities like Phoenix and Tucson, which is helpful for exploring urban areas.

Accommodation Options

From posh resorts in Scottsdale and Sedona with spas and breathtaking vistas to more affordable hotels and motels, Arizona has it all when it comes to accommodations. Many cottages and campers are located close to parks and popular hiking routes, perfect for those who enjoy spending time in nature. It is recommended to make an advance reservation, particularly during busy tourist seasons or when there are major local events planned.

Safety and Health Tips

Tourists visiting Arizona should drink plenty of water and wear sunscreen because of the state's arid climate. Always remember to bring plenty of water, sunscreen, and a hat on a hike. Keep your distance from dangerous creatures and be wary of snakes and scorpions. Because of the unpredictable nature of weather, especially during the monsoon season (June–September), it is wise to check the forecast before venturing outdoors.

Local Customs and Etiquette

It is extremely important to respect the local traditions and history, especially in areas where there are large Native American populations. When visiting cultural sites or tribal territory, it is important to be respectful, observe the rules, and get permission before taking pictures. The quality of your vacation experience is enhanced and mutual understanding is fostered via this regard.

Must-Have Travel Gear

Wearing sturdy footwear, a hat, and sunglasses with UV protection is essential for an Arizona trip, whether you're exploring natural landscapes or cities. Daytime and nighttime temperatures might fluctuate greatly, so it's wise to dress in layers during different seasons.

Budget Planning

Depending on your budget, you can choose from a variety of activities in Arizona. Affordable recreational alternatives include city parks and national and state parks, while cultural activities like museum visits and public events are sometimes free or very inexpensive. Preparing a budget in advance will help you keep costs in check and make the process less stressful.

Chapter 8: Exclusive Itineraries for Unique Adventures

Grand Arizona Explorer: A 7-Day Premium Itinerary for Landscape Enthusiasts

Day 1: Arrival in Phoenix, Travel to Sedona

- **Travel Time:** *Approximately 2 hours drive.*
- **Accommodation:** *L'Auberge de Sedona - $450/night; Sedona Rouge Hotel and Spa - $300/night.*
- **Dining:** *Breakfast at Matt's Big Breakfast in Phoenix ($20), lunch at Mariposa Latin Inspired Grill in Sedona ($35), dinner at Elote Cafe ($50).*
- **Activities:** *Afternoon guided tour of Sedona's vortex sites - $100, 3 hours; evening photography workshop capturing Sedona's red rocks - $75, 2 hours.*
- **Daily Costs:** *Min $625, Max $730.*

Day 2: Sedona Exploration

- **Travel Time:** *Travel within Sedona.*
- **Accommodation:** *Same as Day 1.*
- **Dining:** *Breakfast at Coffee Pot Restaurant ($15), lunch at The Hudson ($30), dinner at Rene at Tlaquepaque ($60).*

- **Activities:** *Morning hot air balloon ride over Sedona - $250, 3 hours; afternoon spa session at Sedona's New Day Spa - $200, 2 hours.*
- **Daily Costs:** *Min $700, Max $1,000.*

Day 3: Sedona to Grand Canyon South Rim

- **Travel Time:** *2 hours drive.*
- **Accommodation:** *El Tovar Hotel - $300/night; Bright Angel Lodge - $200/night.*
- **Dining:** *Breakfast at Indian Gardens Cafe ($20), lunch at El Tovar Dining Room ($40), dinner at Arizona Room ($50).*
- **Activities:** *Guided geological tour of the Grand Canyon - $150, 4 hours; sunset helicopter tour over the Canyon - $300, 2 hours.*
- **Daily Costs:** *Min $810, Max $940.*

Day 4: Exploring Grand Canyon

- **Travel Time:** *Minimal; moving between South Rim sites.*
- **Accommodation:** *Same as Day 3.*
- **Dining:** *Breakfast at Bright Angel Restaurant ($20), lunch packed by Phantom Ranch ($25), dinner at Bright Angel Lodge ($50).*
- **Activities:** *Full day guided hike to Plateau Point - $200, 8 hours; star gazing program at the Grand Canyon - $50, 2 hours.*
- **Daily Costs:** *Min $595, Max $625.*

Day 5: Grand Canyon to Page

- **Travel Time:** *2.5 hours drive.*
- **Accommodation:** *Amangiri - $1800/night; Lake Powell Resort - $250/night.*
- **Dining:** *Breakfast at El Tovar ($25), lunch at Driftwood Lounge ($35), dinner at Bonkers Restaurant in Page ($45).*
- **Activities:** *Tour of Antelope Canyon - $120, 2 hours; private boat tour on Lake Powell - $400, 4 hours.*
- **Daily Costs:** *Min $2,425, Max $3,255.*

Day 6: Page to Flagstaff

- **Travel Time:** *2 hours drive.*
- **Accommodation:** *Little America Hotel - $180/night; Weatherford Hotel - $130/night.*

- **Dining:** *Breakfast at Canyon Crepes Cafe ($20), lunch at Big John's Texas BBQ ($30), dinner at Brix Restaurant and Wine Bar ($60).*
- **Activities:** *Morning kayak trip on Lake Powell - $150, 4 hours; visit to Wupatki National Monument - $15, 2 hours.*
- **Daily Costs:** *Min $395, Max $545.*

Day 7: Flagstaff back to Phoenix

- **Travel Time:** *2 hours drive back to Phoenix.*
- **Accommodation:** *None required as departure day.*
- **Dining:** *Breakfast at Macy's European Coffeehouse in Flagstaff ($15), lunch at Postino WineCafe in Phoenix ($30), early dinner at Chelsea's Kitchen ($40).*
- **Activities:** *Morning hike in Coconino National Forest - $20, 3 hours; afternoon tour of the Musical Instrument Museum in Phoenix - $25, 3 hours.*
- **Daily Costs:** *Min $130, Max $170.*

Total 7-Day Costs:

- **Minimum Total Cost:** *$4,880 per person.*
- **Maximum Total Cost:** *$6,375 per person.*

This premium itinerary for Arizona offers an in-depth exploration of its most iconic landscapes, combining luxurious accommodations, gourmet dining, and unique, high-budget activities. From the spiritual energy of Sedona to the majestic vastness of the Grand Canyon, and the serene waters of Lake Powell, each day unfolds as a new chapter in an unforgettable adventure, designed to awe and inspire. Whether soaring above Sedona in a hot air balloon, hiking beneath the rim of the

Arizona Spectacular: A 7-Day Itinerary for Scenic Lovers on a Budget

Day 1: Phoenix to Sedona

- **Travel Time:** *Approximately 2 hours by car.*
- **Accommodation:** *Sky Ranch Lodge - $120/night; Rancho Sedona RV Park - $45/night.*
- **Dining:** *Breakfast at Matt's Big Breakfast, Phoenix ($10), lunch at Sedona Memories Bakery Cafe ($12), dinner at Tortas de Fuego, Sedona ($15).*

- **Activities:** *Visit to Montezuma Castle National Monument - $10, 1 hour; evening stargazing tour - $15, 2 hours.*
- **Daily Costs:** *Min $102, Max $172.*

Day 2: Exploring Sedona

- **Travel Time:** *Minimal, exploring local area.*
- **Accommodation:** *Same as Day 1.*
- **Dining:** *Breakfast at Coffee Pot Restaurant ($10), packed lunch from Whole Foods Market ($10), dinner at Oaxaca Restaurant ($20).*
- **Activities:** *Morning hike at Cathedral Rock - Free, 3 hours; afternoon jeep tour to Bell Rock - $85, 2 hours.*
- **Daily Costs:** *Min $90, Max $245.*

Day 3: Sedona to Grand Canyon South Rim

- **Travel Time:** *2.5 hours drive.*
- **Accommodation:** *Mather Campground - $18/night; Red Feather Lodge - $90/night.*
- **Dining:** *Breakfast at Red Rock Cafe ($10), packed lunch from Safeway ($8), dinner at El Tovar Dining Room ($30).*
- **Activities:** *South Rim walking tour - Free, duration varies; Ranger-led sunset talk - Free, 1 hour.*
- **Daily Costs:** *Min $66, Max $173.*

Day 4: Grand Canyon Exploration

- **Travel Time:** *Traveling between viewpoints within the park.*
- **Accommodation:** *Same as Day 3.*
- **Dining:** *Breakfast at Bright Angel Bicycles and Cafe ($8), lunch at Maswik Pizza Pub ($15), dinner at Yavapai Tavern ($20).*
- **Activities:** *Morning hike down Bright Angel Trail - Free, 4 hours; afternoon rafting on the Colorado River - $150, 3 hours.*
- **Daily Costs:** *Min $61, Max $283.*

Day 5: Grand Canyon to Page

- **Travel Time:** *2.5 hours drive.*
- **Accommodation:** *Page Boy Motel - $70/night; Lake Powell Campground - $25/night.*
- **Dining:** *Breakfast at Canyon Village Market ($5), lunch at BirdHouse ($10), dinner at Big John's Texas BBQ ($20).*

- **Activities:** *Visit to Horseshoe Bend - Free, 2 hours; Kayak rental on Lake Powell - $40, half-day.*
- **Daily Costs:** *Min $100, Max $155.*

Day 6: Page to Flagstaff

- **Travel Time:** *2 hours drive.*
- **Accommodation:** *Canyon Inn Hotel - $90/night; Woody Mountain Campground - $30/night.*
- **Dining:** *Breakfast at Ranch House Grille ($10), lunch packed from Safeway ($6), dinner at Historic Brewing Company ($20).*
- **Activities:** *Antelope Canyon tour - $48, 1.5 hours; evening visit to Walnut Canyon National Monument - $15, 2 hours.*
- **Daily Costs:** *Min $89, Max $209.*

Day 7: Flagstaff back to Phoenix

- **Travel Time:** *2 hours drive back to Phoenix.*
- **Accommodation:** *N/A for the departure day.*
- **Dining:** *Breakfast at Brandy's Restaurant, Flagstaff ($10), lunch at Cornish Pasty Co, Phoenix ($12), early dinner at airport ($15).*
- **Activities:** *Morning hike at Coconino National Forest - Free, 3 hours; visit to the Arizona Science Center - $20, 4 hours.*
- **Daily Costs:** *Min $57, Max $77.*

Total 7-Day Costs:

- **Minimum Total Cost:** *$565 per person.*
- **Maximum Total Cost:** *$1,364 per person.*

This itinerary offers an enchanting journey through Arizona's most scenic landscapes, tailored for travelers seeking both adventure and tranquility without straining their wallets. From the red rocks of Sedona to the majestic Grand Canyon, and the serene waters of Lake Powell, this trip promises a memorable exploration of natural wonders, ideal for photographers, hikers, and anyone looking to immerse themselves in breathtaking views. Each day is filled with engaging activities that highlight the unique beauty of Arizona, ensuring an unforgettable experience at an accessible price.

Arizona Natural Wonders: A 7-Day Premium Itinerary for the Adventurous Spirit

Day 1: Arrival in Phoenix, Drive to Sedona

- **Travel Time:** *2 hours from Phoenix to Sedona.*
- **Accommodation:** *L'Auberge de Sedona - $400/night; Sedona Rouge Hotel and Spa - $250/night.*
- **Dining:** *Breakfast at Phoenix Sky Harbor ($15), lunch at The Hudson, Sedona ($30), dinner at Mariposa ($50).*
- **Activities:** *Guided Red Rock Jeep tour - $95, 2 hours; Evening meditation retreat - $85, 1.5 hours.*
- **Daily Costs:** *Min $580, Max $680.*

Day 2: Full Day in Sedona

- **Travel Time:** *Minimal; local exploration.*
- **Accommodation:** *Same as Day 1.*
- **Dining:** *Breakfast at Coffee Pot Restaurant ($15), lunch at ChocolaTree Organic Eatery ($25), dinner at Dahl & Di Luca Ristorante Italiano ($45).*
- **Activities:** *Morning hot air balloon ride - $225, 3 hours; Afternoon guided hike in Boynton Canyon - $75, 3 hours.*
- **Daily Costs:** *Min $685, Max $810.*

Day 3: Sedona to Grand Canyon South Rim

- **Travel Time:** *2.5 hours.*
- **Accommodation:** *El Tovar Hotel - $300/night; Bright Angel Lodge - $200/night.*
- **Dining:** *Breakfast at Indian Gardens Cafe ($20), packed lunch from Safeway ($15), dinner at El Tovar Dining Room ($50).*
- **Activities:** *Guided Rim Trail walk - Free, 3 hours; Sunset wildlife safari - $150, 2 hours.*
- **Daily Costs:** *Min $585, Max $735.*

Day 4: Grand Canyon Adventures

- **Travel Time:** *Minimal; traveling within the park.*
- **Accommodation:** *Same as Day 3.*
- **Dining:** *Breakfast at Canyon Village Market ($15), lunch at Arizona Room ($30), dinner at Phantom Ranch ($45).*

- **Activities:** *Early morning mule ride to Plateau Point - $155, 5 hours; Evening stargazing with a ranger - $50, 2 hours.*
- **Daily Costs:** *Min $495, Max $675.*

Day 5: Grand Canyon to Page

- **Travel Time:** *2.5 hours to Page.*
- **Accommodation:** *Lake Powell Resorts - $250/night; Amangiri - $1800/night.*
- **Dining:** *Breakfast at El Tovar ($25), lunch at BirdHouse ($20), dinner at Into The Grand ($40).*
- **Activities:** *Antelope Canyon photography tour - $120, 2 hours; Lake Powell kayak excursion - $95, half-day.*
- **Daily Costs:** *Min $550, Max $2,235.*

Day 6: Page to Flagstaff

- **Travel Time:** *2 hours.*
- **Accommodation:** *Little America Hotel - $150/night; Weatherford Hotel - $120/night.*
- **Dining:** *Breakfast at Canyon Crepes Cafe ($15), lunch at Big John's Texas BBQ ($20), dinner at Brix Restaurant and Wine Bar ($50).*
- **Activities:** *Guided hike at Monument Valley - $180, 4 hours; Visit to Navajo National Monument - $15, 2 hours.*
- **Daily Costs:** *Min $530, Max $615.*

Day 7: Flagstaff to Phoenix

- **Travel Time:** *2 hours drive back to Phoenix.*
- **Accommodation:** *None needed, as it's a departure day.*
- **Dining:** *Breakfast at MartAnne's Breakfast Palace, Flagstaff ($20), lunch at Postino WineCafe, Phoenix ($25), early dinner at Chelsea's Kitchen, Phoenix ($40).*
- **Activities:** *Morning visit to Walnut Canyon - $15, 2 hours; Afternoon leisure time at Desert Botanical Garden, Phoenix - $25, 3 hours.*
- **Daily Costs:** *Min $125, Max $145.*

Total 7-Day Costs:

- **Minimum Total Cost:** *$3,070 per person.*
- **Maximum Total Cost:** *$6,295 per person.*

This expertly curated itinerary is designed to let you immerse yourself in the majestic landscapes of Arizona, combining luxury and adventure. From the spiritual vistas of Sedona to the grandeur of the Grand Canyon and the serene beauty of Lake Powell, each day is structured to provide an unforgettable experience with comfortable accommodations, exquisite dining, and thrilling activities. Enjoy the natural splendor of Arizona with the comfort of knowing every detail has been carefully planned to enhance your journey.

Arizona's Natural Charm: A 7-Day Itinerary for Budget-Conscious Adventurers

Day 1: Phoenix to Sedona

- **Travel Time:** *2 hours drive.*
- **Accommodation:** *Rancho Sedona RV Park - $45/night; Sedona Village Lodge - $85/night.*
- **Dining:** *Breakfast at Welcome Diner in Phoenix ($8), lunch at Sedona Memories Bakery Cafe ($10), dinner at Picazzo's Healthy Italian Kitchen ($20).*
- **Activities:** *Visit Montezuma Castle National Monument - $10, 1 hour; Evening hike at Airport Mesa - Free, 2 hours.*
- **Daily Costs:** *Min $83, Max $133.*

Day 2: Sedona Exploration

- **Travel Time:** *Minimal; local area exploration.*
- **Accommodation:** *Same as Day 1.*
- **Dining:** *Breakfast at Coffee Pot Restaurant ($10), packed lunch from Whole Foods Market ($12), dinner at ChocolaTree Organic Oasis ($18).*
- **Activities:** *Guided Cathedral Rock hike - $65, 3 hours; Oak Creek Canyon scenic drive - Free, duration varies.*
- **Daily Costs:** *Min $150, Max $180.*

Day 3: Sedona to Grand Canyon South Rim

- **Travel Time:** *2.5 hours.*
- **Accommodation:** *Mather Campground - $18/night; Yavapai Lodge - $90/night.*
- **Dining:** *Breakfast at Indian Gardens Cafe ($15), lunch packed from Basha's ($6), dinner at Maswik Cafeteria ($15).*

- **Activities:** *Grand Canyon Village walking tour - Free, duration varies; Ranger-led sunset talk at Yavapai Point - Free, 1 hour.*
- **Daily Costs:** *Min $54, Max $126.*

Day 4: Grand Canyon Exploration

- **Travel Time:** *Minimal; exploring park areas.*
- **Accommodation:** *Same as Day 3.*
- **Dining:** *Breakfast at Bright Angel Bicycles and Cafe ($10), lunch at El Tovar Dining Room ($20), dinner cooked at campsite ($5).*
- **Activities:** *South Kaibab Trail hike to Cedar Ridge - Free, 3 hours; Grand Canyon IMAX experience - $14, 1 hour.*
- **Daily Costs:** *Min $57, Max $129.*

Day 5: Grand Canyon to Page

- **Travel Time:** *2.5 hours.*
- **Accommodation:** *Wahweap Campground - $30/night; Page Boy Motel - $80/night.*
- **Dining:** *Breakfast at El Tovar ($20), lunch at Big John's Texas BBQ ($15), dinner at State 48 Tavern ($25).*
- **Activities:** *Horseshoe Bend visit - $10, 2 hours; Glen Canyon Dam tour - $5, 1 hour.*
- **Daily Costs:** *Min $100, Max $165.*

Day 6: Page to Flagstaff

- **Travel Time:** *2 hours.*
- **Accommodation:** *Woody Mountain Campground - $30/night; Canyon Inn Hotel - $90/night.*
- **Dining:** *Breakfast at Ranch House Grille ($10), packed lunch from Walmart ($7), dinner at Lumberyard Brewing Co. ($20).*
- **Activities:** *Antelope Canyon lower tour - $40, 1 hour; Lake Powell boat rental for half-day - $150, 4 hours.*
- **Daily Costs:** *Min $217, Max $307.*

Day 7: Flagstaff to Phoenix

- **Travel Time:** *2 hours drive back to Phoenix.*
- **Accommodation:** *None required as it's a departure day.*
- **Dining:** *Breakfast at MartAnne's Burrito Palace, Flagstaff ($12), lunch at Joyride Taco House, Phoenix ($15), early dinner at In-N-Out Burger ($8).*

- **Activities:** *Walnut Canyon National Monument hike - $15, 2 hours; Arizona Science Center visit - $20, 3 hours.*
- **Daily Costs:** *Min $70, Max $70.*

Total 7-Day Costs:

- **Minimum Total Cost:** *$741 per person.*
- **Maximum Total Cost:** *$1,160 per person.*

This itinerary offers a mix of guided tours, self-driven exploration, and immersive experiences in nature across Arizona's most iconic landscapes, tailored for those with a medium to low budget. From the spiritual red rocks of Sedona to the awe-inspiring grandeur of the Grand Canyon and the serene waters of Lake Powell, each day brings a new adventure, ensuring you experience the best of Arizona without breaking the bank. This journey promises memorable moments, whether you're hiking scenic trails, exploring historic sites, or simply soaking in the natural beauty of the Southwest.

Arizona Family Adventure: A 7-Day Journey for Families with Children Aged 6-12

Day 1: Arrival in Phoenix, Drive to Tucson

- **Travel Time:** *Approximately 2 hours.*
- **Accommodation:** *Arizona Inn - $140/night; Tucson Marriott University Park - $110/night.*
- **Dining:** *Breakfast at Matt's Big Breakfast in Phoenix ($12), lunch at Hub Restaurant & Ice Creamery in Tucson ($15), dinner at Reilly's Pizza & Drink ($20).*
- **Activities:** *Visit the Arizona Science Center in Phoenix - $18, 2 hours; Explore Children's Museum Tucson - $9, 2 hours.*
- **Daily Costs:** *Min $194, Max $224.*

Day 2: Exploring Tucson

- **Travel Time:** *Minimal; local city travel.*
- **Accommodation:** *Same as Day 1.*
- **Dining:** *Breakfast at Hotel Congress ($10), lunch at Zinburger ($12), dinner at Poco & Mom's Cantina ($18).*
- **Activities:** *Morning at Reid Park Zoo - $10.50, 3 hours; Afternoon visit to Saguaro National Park East - $20 per vehicle, duration varies.*

- **Daily Costs:** *Min $160.5, Max $190.5.*

Day 3: Tucson to Bisbee

- **Travel Time:** *1.5 hours.*
- **Accommodation:** *Copper Queen Hotel - $100/night; The School House Inn Bed & Breakfast - $80/night.*
- **Dining:** *Breakfast at Bisbee Breakfast Club ($12), lunch at High Desert Market and Café ($10), dinner at Santiago's Mexican Restaurant ($20).*
- **Activities:** *Bisbee Mining & Historical Museum - $8, 1.5 hours; Queen Mine Tour - $14, 1 hour.*
- **Daily Costs:** *Min $134, Max $164.*

Day 4: Bisbee to Flagstaff

- **Travel Time:** *4.5 hours.*
- **Accommodation:** *Little America Hotel - $150/night; Drury Inn & Suites Flagstaff - $130/night.*
- **Dining:** *Breakfast at Bisbee Coffee Company ($10), lunch at Historic Brewing Company ($15), dinner at Fat Olives ($25).*
- **Activities:** *Explore the Meteor Crater Natural Landmark - $18, 1.5 hours; Visit Lowell Observatory for evening stargazing - $17, 2 hours.*
- **Daily Costs:** *Min $220, Max $250.*

Day 5: Flagstaff to Grand Canyon

- **Travel Time:** *1.5 hours.*
- **Accommodation:** *Yavapai Lodge - $180/night; Mather Campground - $18/night.*
- **Dining:** *Breakfast at Macy's European Coffeehouse ($12), lunch at Maswik Cafeteria ($15), dinner cooked at campsite ($10).*
- **Activities:** *Grand Canyon Junior Ranger Program - Free, duration varies; IMAX movie at the National Geographic Visitor Center - $14, 45 minutes.*
- **Daily Costs:** *Min $239, Max $409.*

Day 6: Grand Canyon to Sedona

- **Travel Time:** *2.5 hours.*
- **Accommodation:** *Arabella Hotel Sedona - $150/night; Sugar Loaf Lodge - $90/night.*

- **Dining:** *Breakfast at Canyon Village Market ($10), lunch at Slide Rock Market ($12), dinner at Oaxaca Restaurant ($20).*
- **Activities:** *Slide Rock State Park - $20 per vehicle, duration varies; Evening Pink Jeep Tours at Sedona - $95, 2 hours.*
- **Daily Costs:** *Min $197, Max $277.*

Day 7: Sedona to Phoenix

- **Travel Time:** *2 hours.*
- **Accommodation:** *None needed, as it's a departure day.*
- **Dining:** *Breakfast at Coffee Pot Restaurant ($12), lunch at Rock Springs Café ($15), early dinner at Chelsea's Kitchen ($25).*
- **Activities:** *Morning hike at Red Rock State Park - $7, 2 hours; Visit to the Butterfly Wonderland in Scottsdale - $23, 2 hours.*
- **Daily Costs:** *Min $82, Max $92.*

Total 7-Day Costs:

- **Minimum Total Cost:** *$1,226.5 per person.*
- **Maximum Total Cost:** *$1,811.5 per person.*

This thoughtfully designed 7-day itinerary is perfect for families eager to explore Arizona's stunning landscapes, rich history, and engaging attractions. Each day offers new adventures that are both child-friendly and educational, from touching the clouds in a pink jeep tour to becoming a Junior Ranger at the Grand Canyon. Dive into this family-friendly adventure and create memories that will last a lifetime.

Discover Arizona's Rich Tapestry: A 7-Day Cultural Itinerary

Day 1: Arrival in Phoenix, Travel to Tucson

- **Travel Time:** *Approximately 2 hours by car.*
- **Accommodation:** *Hotel Congress - $120/night; The Downtown Clifton - $100/night.*
- **Dining:** *Breakfast at Matt's Big Breakfast, Phoenix ($15), lunch at El Charro Café, Tucson ($20), dinner at Café Poca Cosa ($30).*
- **Activities:** *Visit the Heard Museum - $18, 2 hours; evening walking tour of Historic Downtown Tucson - $15, 1.5 hours.*
- **Daily Costs:** *Min $198, Max $223.*

Day 2: Tucson Explorations

- **Travel Time:** *Minimal; local city travel.*
- **Accommodation:** *Same as Day 1.*
- **Dining:** *Breakfast at Cup Café in Hotel Congress ($15), lunch at The Little One ($12), dinner at Penca ($25).*
- **Activities:** *Tour Mission San Xavier del Bac - Free, 1 hour; Arizona State Museum visit - $10, 2 hours.*
- **Daily Costs:** *Min $162, Max $187.*

Day 3: Tucson to Globe

- **Travel Time:** *2.5 hours.*
- **Accommodation:** *Dream Manor Inn - $110/night; Belle-Aire Motel - $70/night.*
- **Dining:** *Breakfast at Frank's/Francisco's ($10), lunch at Besh Ba Gowah Café ($12), dinner at Guayo's El Rey ($20).*
- **Activities:** *Explore Besh Ba Gowah Archaeological Park - $5, 2 hours; tour of Old Dominion Historic Mine Park - $5, 1.5 hours.*
- **Daily Costs:** *Min $122, Max $162.*

Day 4: Globe to Flagstaff

- **Travel Time:** *3.5 hours.*
- **Accommodation:** *Monte Vista Hotel - $130/night; Weatherford Hotel - $90/night.*
- **Dining:** *Breakfast at Chalo's Casa Reynoso ($10), lunch at MartAnne's Breakfast Palace ($15), dinner at Diablo Burger ($25).*
- **Activities:** *Visit the Museum of Northern Arizona - $12, 2 hours; Navajo Nation Reservation cultural tour - $50, 3 hours.*
- **Daily Costs:** *Min $232, Max $272.*

Day 5: Flagstaff to Grand Canyon

- **Travel Time:** *1.5 hours.*
- **Accommodation:** *Yavapai Lodge - $150/night; Mather Campground - $18/night.*
- **Dining:** *Breakfast at Late for the Train ($12), lunch at El Tovar Dining Room ($30), dinner cooked at campsite ($10).*
- **Activities:** *Grand Canyon Village historic walk - Free, 2 hours; Evening ranger talk about Native American history at the Canyon - $10, 1 hour.*
- **Daily Costs:** *Min $220, Max $252.*

Day 6: Grand Canyon to Sedona

- **Travel Time:** *2.5 hours.*
- **Accommodation:** *Arabella Hotel Sedona - $150/night; Rancho Sedona RV Park - $45/night.*
- **Dining:** *Breakfast at Bright Angel Restaurant ($15), lunch at Wildflower Bread Company ($18), dinner at Mariposa Latin Inspired Grill ($35).*
- **Activities:** *Visit Palatki Heritage Site - $10, 2 hours; guided tour of Sedona's ancient rock art sites - $25, 2 hours.*
- **Daily Costs:** *Min $243, Max $288.*

Day 7: Sedona back to Phoenix

- **Travel Time:** *2 hours.*
- **Accommodation:** *None needed, as it's a departure day.*
- **Dining:** *Breakfast at Coffee Pot Restaurant ($12), lunch at Sedona Memories Bakery Cafe ($15), early dinner at Pizzeria Bianco, Phoenix ($30).*
- **Activities:** *Morning hike at Vortex sites with cultural storytelling - $20, 2 hours; Visit to Pueblo Grande Museum - $10, 1.5 hours.*
- **Daily Costs:** *Min $87, Max $102.*

Total 7-Day Costs:

- **Minimum Total Cost:** *$1,164 per person.*
- **Maximum Total Cost:** *$1,282 per person.*

This itinerary is crafted to immerse you in the rich cultural and historical tapestry of Arizona, from the vibrant arts and historical scenes of Tucson to the sacred landscapes and stories of the Native American peoples. Each day blends educational visits with firsthand experiences, offering a comprehensive view of Arizona's indigenous heritage and colonial past, all while keeping budget considerations in mind. Explore, learn, and connect with the deep-rooted history that Arizona offers.

Arizona Romance Road: A 7-Day Itinerary for Couples Seeking Magic and Memories

Day 1: Phoenix to Sedona

- **Travel Time:** *Approximately 2 hours by car.*

- **Accommodation:** L'Auberge de Sedona - $300/night; Arabella Hotel Sedona - $200/night.
- **Dining:** Breakfast at Matt's Big Breakfast, Phoenix ($15), lunch at Creekside Sedona ($25), dinner at Mariposa Latin Inspired Grill ($50).
- **Activities:** Afternoon stroll through Tlaquepaque Arts & Shopping Village - Free, duration varies; Sunset jeep tour in Sedona - $85 per person, 2 hours.
- **Daily Costs:** Min $375, Max $475.

Day 2: Exploring Sedona

- **Travel Time:** Minimal; exploring local area.
- **Accommodation:** Same as Day 1.
- **Dining:** Breakfast at Sedona Memories Bakery Cafe ($12), lunch at The Hudson ($20), dinner at Dahl & Di Luca Ristorante Italiano ($40).
- **Activities:** Morning hot air balloon ride - $225 per person, 3 hours; Couples spa treatment at Sedona's New Day Spa - $300 for couples, 2 hours.
- **Daily Costs:** Min $597, Max $697.

Day 3: Sedona to Grand Canyon

- **Travel Time:** 2.5 hours.
- **Accommodation:** Bright Angel Lodge - $150/night; Yavapai Lodge - $120/night.
- **Dining:** Breakfast at Indian Gardens Cafe ($15), packed lunch from Sedona ($10), dinner at El Tovar Dining Room ($50).
- **Activities:** Afternoon Grand Canyon Rim walk - Free, duration varies; Star gazing session near the canyon - $30, 2 hours.
- **Daily Costs:** Min $255, Max $285.

Day 4: Grand Canyon to Page

- **Travel Time:** 2.5 hours.
- **Accommodation:** Lake Powell Resort - $250/night; Courtyard Page at Lake Powell - $150/night.
- **Dining:** Breakfast at Bright Angel Café ($15), lunch at Lake Powell Pizzeria ($15), dinner at Into the Grand ($30).
- **Activities:** Visit to Horseshoe Bend - $10 per person, 1 hour; Private boat tour on Lake Powell - $200 for couples, 4 hours.

- **Daily Costs:** *Min $420, Max $520.*

Day 5: Page to Flagstaff

- **Travel Time:** *2 hours.*
- **Accommodation:** *Little America Hotel - $180/night; Hotel Monte Vista - $130/night.*
- **Dining:** *Breakfast at Ranch House Grille ($12), lunch at Satchmo's ($15), dinner at Brix Restaurant and Wine Bar ($40).*
- **Activities:** *Morning kayak excursion on Lake Powell - $75 per person, 3 hours; Evening at Lowell Observatory - $22 per person, 2 hours.*
- **Daily Costs:** *Min $334, Max $384.*

Day 6: Flagstaff to Jerome

- **Travel Time:** *1 hour.*
- **Accommodation:** *Jerome Grand Hotel - $220/night; Connor Hotel - $160/night.*
- **Dining:** *Breakfast at Brandy's Restaurant ($12), lunch at Haunted Hamburger ($15), dinner at Asylum Restaurant ($45).*
- **Activities:** *Jerome historic ghost town tour - $25 per person, 1.5 hours; Wine tasting at Caduceus Cellars - $20 per person, 1 hour.*
- **Daily Costs:** *Min $307, Max $357.*

Day 7: Jerome to Phoenix

- **Travel Time:** *2 hours.*
- **Accommodation:** *None needed, as it's a departure day.*
- **Dining:** *Breakfast at Flatiron Café ($10), lunch at Rock Springs Café ($15), early dinner at The Arrogant Butcher, Phoenix ($30).*
- **Activities:** *Morning exploration of Jerome State Historic Park - $7, 1.5 hours; Visit to the Musical Instrument Museum in Phoenix - $20, 3 hours.*
- **Daily Costs:** *Min $82, Max $82.*

Total 7-Day Costs:

- **Minimum Total Cost:** *$2,070 per person.*
- **Maximum Total Cost:** *$2,498 per person.*

This itinerary is crafted with love for couples who seek romance and unforgettable experiences across Arizona's vibrant landscapes and historic towns. Each day offers a blend of adventure, relaxation, and romantic moments, perfect for creating cherished memories together. Whether it's soaring above Sedona's red rocks, gazing at stars over the Grand Canyon, or toasting on a sunset cruise on Lake Powell, this journey promises magic at every turn.

Conclusion

As you wind down this book, keep in mind that Arizona is more than just a place—it's an experience waiting to be had. We believe that by delving into the varied landscapes and fascinating history of the Grand Canyon State, you will be captivated by its rich history and unique landscapes. Discover the mesmerizing beauty and rich history of Arizona, from the red rocks of Sedona to the overwhelming grandeur of the Grand Canyon and the lively streets of Tucson. No traveler will be disappointed by this one-of-a-kind destination.

Now that you have this information, you are ready to set out on an exciting and romantic excursion. Make use of it to plot out your journey, gain insight into the local culture, and locate those one-of-a-kind spots that will set your pulse racing. Get ready to be captivated by the tales, secrets, and breathtaking sunset colors that Arizona has to offer.

It has been an honor to accompany you on your journey through Arizona. Cheers to traveling the world and always making space for more wonder, to finding the unexpected, and to savoring the moments.

May you have safe travels and unforgettable adventures!

MAPS & IMAGES AT YOUR FINGERTIPS!

Scan the qr code to download your exclusive bonus

Or copy and paste this address into the search bar

rb.gy/42co8r

Made in the USA
Las Vegas, NV
01 December 2024

13075782R00059